Library of
Davidson College

DAVID & CHARLES SOURCES FOR
CONTEMPORARY ISSUES SERIES

THE POPULATION PROBLEM

SERIES EDITOR: *Ben Whitaker*

also in this series

TRADE UNIONS IN GREAT BRITAIN
John Hughes and Harold Pollins

in preparation

BRITISH BROADCASTING
Anthony Smith

EASTERN EUROPE SINCE STALIN
Jonathan Steele

HIGHER EDUCATION
Brian MacArthur

WESTERN EUROPEAN INTEGRATION
Malcolm Crawford and Roger Broad

ANGLO-AMERICAN RELATIONS SINCE THE SECOND WORLD WAR
Ian S. McDonald

THE ELECTORAL SYSTEM
David Butler

THE WELFARE STATE
Geoffrey Smith and E. T. Ashton

PRIVACY
Mervyn Jones

LOCAL GOVERNMENT
Owen A. Hartley

REVOLUTION
Adam Roberts

THE CITY
David C. Thorns

DAVID & CHARLES SOURCES FOR CONTEMPORARY ISSUES SERIES

THE POPULATION PROBLEM

Compiled and Edited by

Stanley Johnson

A HALSTED PRESS BOOK

JOHN WILEY & SONS
New York

© Stanley Johnson 1973

Published in the U.S.A.
by Halsted Press, a Division
of John Wiley & Sons, Inc.
New York

ISBN 0-470-44616-1
Library of Congress Catalog Card Number 73-15140

Printed in Great Britain

Contents

		PAGE
	LIST OF ILLUSTRATIONS	9
	LIST OF TABLES	11
	ACKNOWLEDGEMENT	13
	INTRODUCTION	17

PART ONE: FACTS AND FIGURES AND THEIR MEANING — 34

FERTILITY AND POPULATION GROWTH
1 UN. *Youthfulness of world population* — 34

POPULATION PROJECTIONS
2 UN Population Division. *Comments on total population growth* — 39

INDIVIDUAL RIGHTS
3A UN Declaration. *The family* — 46
3B U Thant. *Family rights* — 46
3C Teheran Conference. *Family rights* — 47

NATIONAL GOALS
4 Dr Norman E. Borlaug. *The green revolution, peace and humanity* — 50

5   World Bank. *Population planning*   59

INTERNATIONAL IMPLICATIONS

6A United Nations Association of the United States. *The population crisis is the world's concern*   61
6B Indira Gandhi. *Life is one and the world is one*   64
7   'The Limits to Growth Report'. *On reaching a state of global equilibrium*   67

PART TWO: THE DEVELOPING WORLD   72

ASIA

8   Han Suyin. *Family Planning in China*   75
9A S. Krishna Kumar. *Vasectomy in India*   81
9B Government of India. *Indian Family Planning*   88

AFRICA

10A Government of Botswana. *Family planning policy*   90
10B Republic of Ghana. *Family planning policy*   91
10C Republic of Kenya. *Family planning policy*   92
11   Dr Francis Olu Okediji. *Sociological background to family life in tropical Africa*   93
12A Tanzania Radio. *Family planning programme*   96
12B Uganda Radio. *Family planning programme*   99

LATIN AMERICA

13   Caracas Meeting on Population Policies. *Declaration* and *General recommendations*   100
14   Former Presidents Camargo and Frei. *Statements*   103

PART THREE: THE DEVELOPED WORLD   105

15   UN. *The developed world in 1970*   105

BRITAIN

16   House of Commons Select Committee on Science and Technology. *Report*   106

USA

17   John D. Rockefeller 3rd. *Letter to President and Congress*   111

18	Commission on Population Growth and the American Future. *Perspective on population*	112
	ROMANIA	
19	Drs Henry P. David and Nichols H. Wright. *Abortion in Romania*	120
20	Pugwash and Environmental Future Conferences. *Statements 1971*	128

PART FOUR: OBSTACLES TO ACTION 130

THE ROMAN CATHOLIC CHURCH

21A	Papal Encyclical. *Humanae Vitae*	130
21B	Dr Leo Alting Von Geusau. *International reaction to the encyclical Humanae Vitae*	140
22	Mrs Judith Hart. *A woman's view*	156

MARXISM

23	Professor B. Z. Urlanis. *Marxism and birth control*	157

ISLAM

24A	Sheikh Abdullah Al-Qalqili. *Fatwa: family planning in Islam*	163
24B	Rabat Conference. *On family planning*	166

PART FIVE: ORGANISATIONS CONCERNED WITH POPULATION PROBLEMS 169

UNITED NATIONS

25A	UN. *Statement of policy on population*	169
25B	UN. *Resolution on population*	171
25C	UN. *Statement by heads of state*	174
26	President Richard M. Nixon. *Message on population*	176
27A	UN. *World population year, 1974*	178
27B	UN. *Recommendation for world population plan of action*	180
28	Philip M. Hauser. *The population dilemma*	180
29	UN. *The work of UNFPA*	181

30	Peterson Report. *Gathering data*	194
31A	UN. *Activities of UNICEF*	195
31B	UN. *UNESCO in the population field*	196
31C	UN. *FAO work in relation to population*	197

OTHER ORGANISATIONS

32	ILO. *Policy on population*	198
33	WHO. *Health and population*	199
34	World Bank. *Assistance for population policies*	201
35	IPPF. *Aims and achievements*	202
36	OECD. *Work on population*	208
37	Population Council. *Aims*	209
38	Rockefeller Foundation. *Work on population*	209
39	Ford Foundation. *Expenditure on population studies*	211
40	IUSSP. *Aims*	212

APPENDICES 1 DEFINITIONS	216
2 THOMAS ROBERT MALTHUS	219
BIBLIOGRAPHY	221
INDEX	225

List of Illustrations

FIGURES

		PAGE
1	Estimated and conjectured trends in birth and death rates, 1750–2000	18
2	Distribution of population, 1830–2000	35
3	World births in percentages by region, 1970	36
4	Trends in food production and population in the developing regions	49
5	School enrolment	52
6	Time relationships between a birth and future service requirements	54
7	Growth of world population and urban population in various categories, 1920–80	55
8	Comparison between developed and less developed world in population and GNP	58
9	GNP growth rate for the four regions of (1) Africa, (2) East Asia, (3) Latin America, and (4) the Near East and South Asia	59
10	Projection for disaster	63

MAP

World fertility patterns — 14–15

List of Tables

		PAGE
1	Estimated and conjectured average annual birth rates, death rates and rates of natural increase for currently more developed and less developed regions 1960–70 and selected periods 1750–2000	20
2	World population increase, 1965–70	36
3	World population, 1970 (mid-year estimates)	38
4	Total population estimates and annual rates of growth by regions, 1965–2000—medium variant	41
5	Total population estimates and annual rates of growth by regions, 1965–2000—high variant	43
6	Total population estimates and annual rates of growth by regions, 1965–2000—low variant	44
7	Total population estimates and annual rates of growth by regions, 1965–2000—constant fertility variant	45
8	Level of unemployment and underemployment in developing countries, excluding mainland China	57
9	Current and ultimate stationary populations on assumption that birth rates drop immediately to stationary level	63
10	Number of countries and distribution of the population in the major regions of the developing world, by governmental position on family planning programs and policies	73

11	Population distribution in millions in developing countries (excluding mainland China) by fertility and mortality levels, 1970	74
12	Assistance for demographic, biomedical and family planning work, by regions, 1969 and 1970	213
13	Assistance to population activities as percentage of total official development assistance, 1969 and 1970	214
14	Resources provided to assist population activities, by region, 1970	215

Acknowledgement

The author gratefully acknowledges the help and co-operation of all those who gave permission for material to be reprinted in this book. Full details of the source of documents, tables, quotations, etc, are given in the text itself.

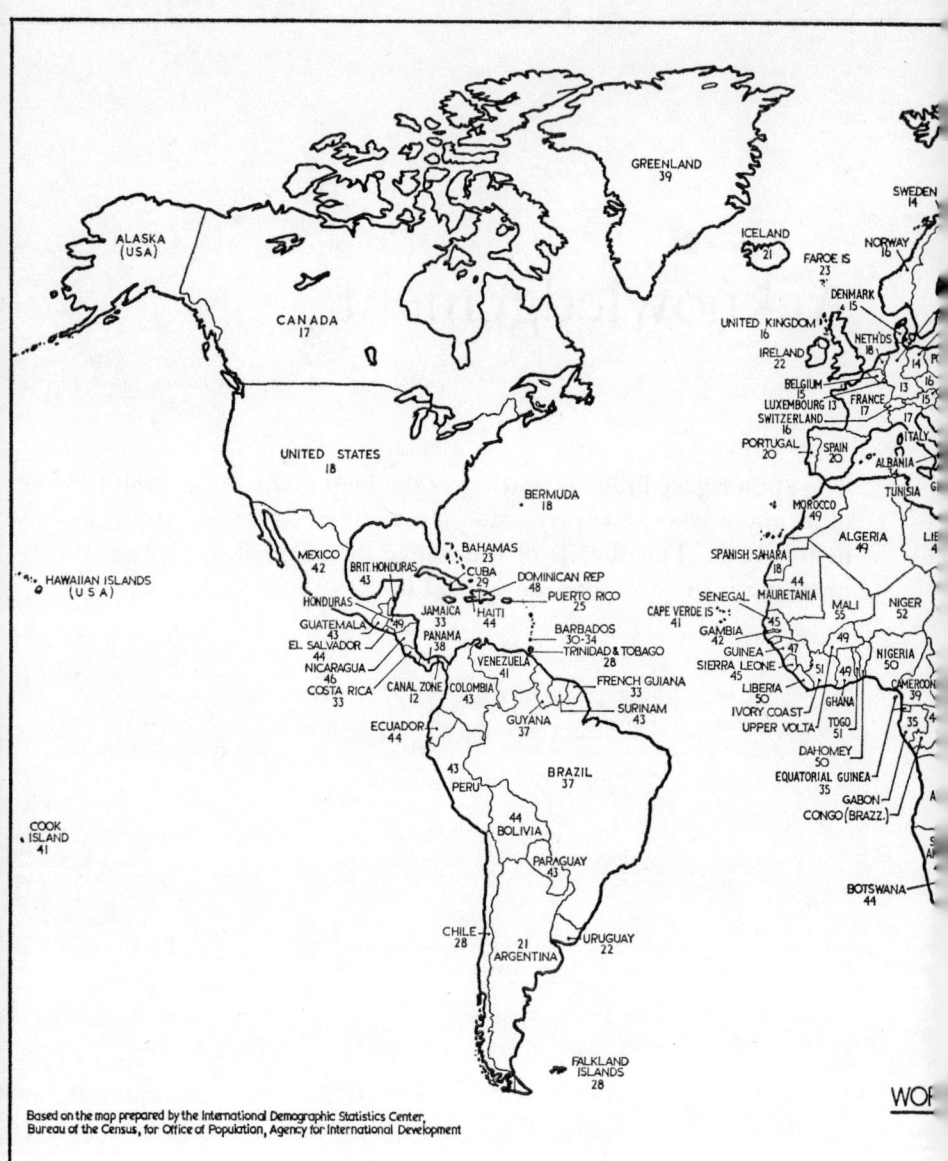

World fertility patterns—1970 or most recent date
(The numbers represent crude birth rate per 1,000)
SOURCE: International Demographic Statistic Center, Bureau of the Census, USA

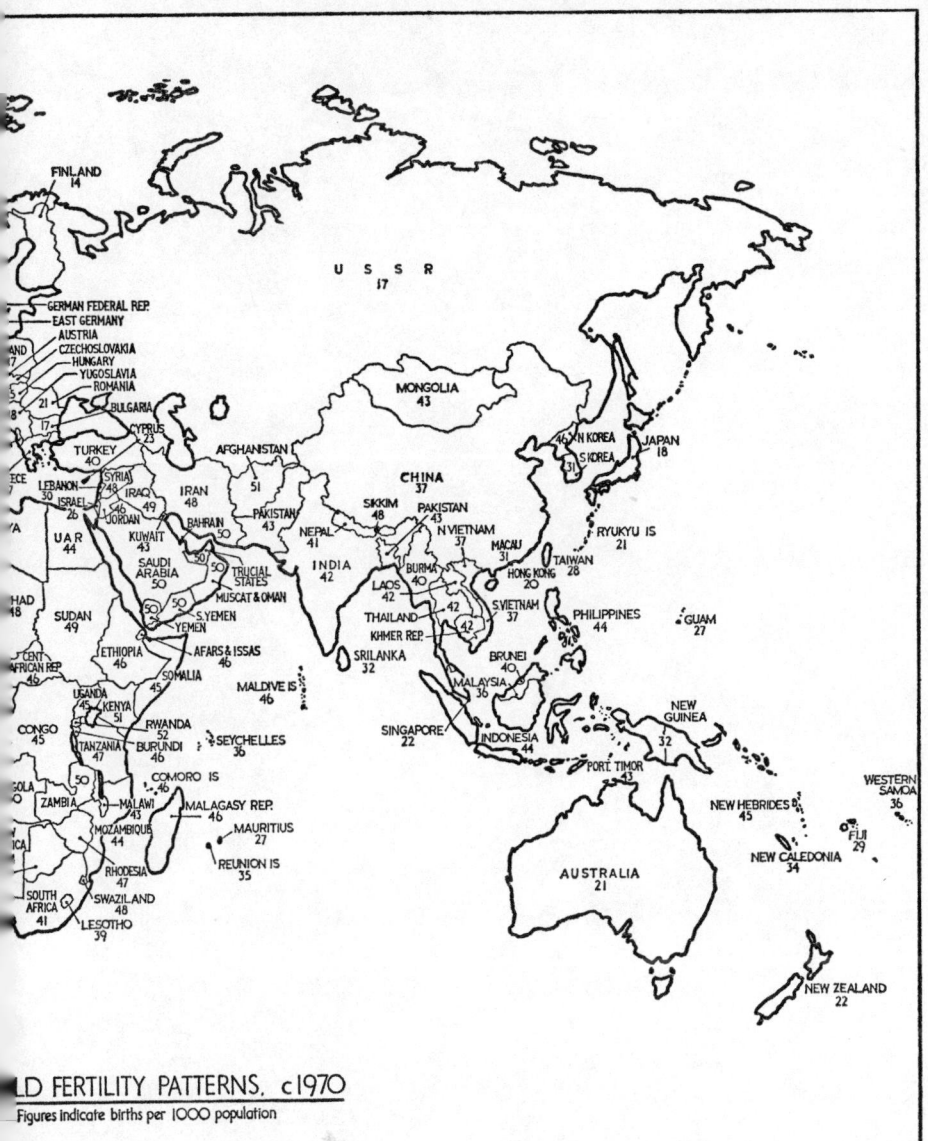

WORLD FERTILITY PATTERNS, c1970
Figures indicate births per 1000 population

Introduction

There seems to be some dispute as to when Man first came into existence. Java Man, called Pithecanthropus, stood upright, had a low flat skull of about 1,000cc capacity (in adult males) and probably appeared around 500,000 years ago. If we take a more technical definition of Man, ie a being having a mean cranial capacity of 1,350cc, an approximately vertical forehead, the presence of a chin eminence, etc, it seems reasonable to assign to *Homo Sapiens* an antiquity of not less than 100,000 years, ie starting some time in the second Interglacial Period. But the fact is, whether it was 500,000 years or only 100,000, it took a very long time indeed for the Earth to acquire its first 1,000 million human beings.

The watershed of the first 1,000 million was very probably reached around the beginning of the 1830s. It took about 100 years to add the second 1,000 million and only 30 years (between 1930 and 1960) to add the third. Today the world's population has reached a total of 3,700 million.

The daily increase in the population of the world at the moment is about 180,000, this figure being the difference between daily births of approximately 320,000 and daily deaths of around 140,000.

Three-quarters of the Earth's inhabitants live in what are euphemistically known as the developing regions, and more than one half of that total is in Asia. In mid-1970 Africa had

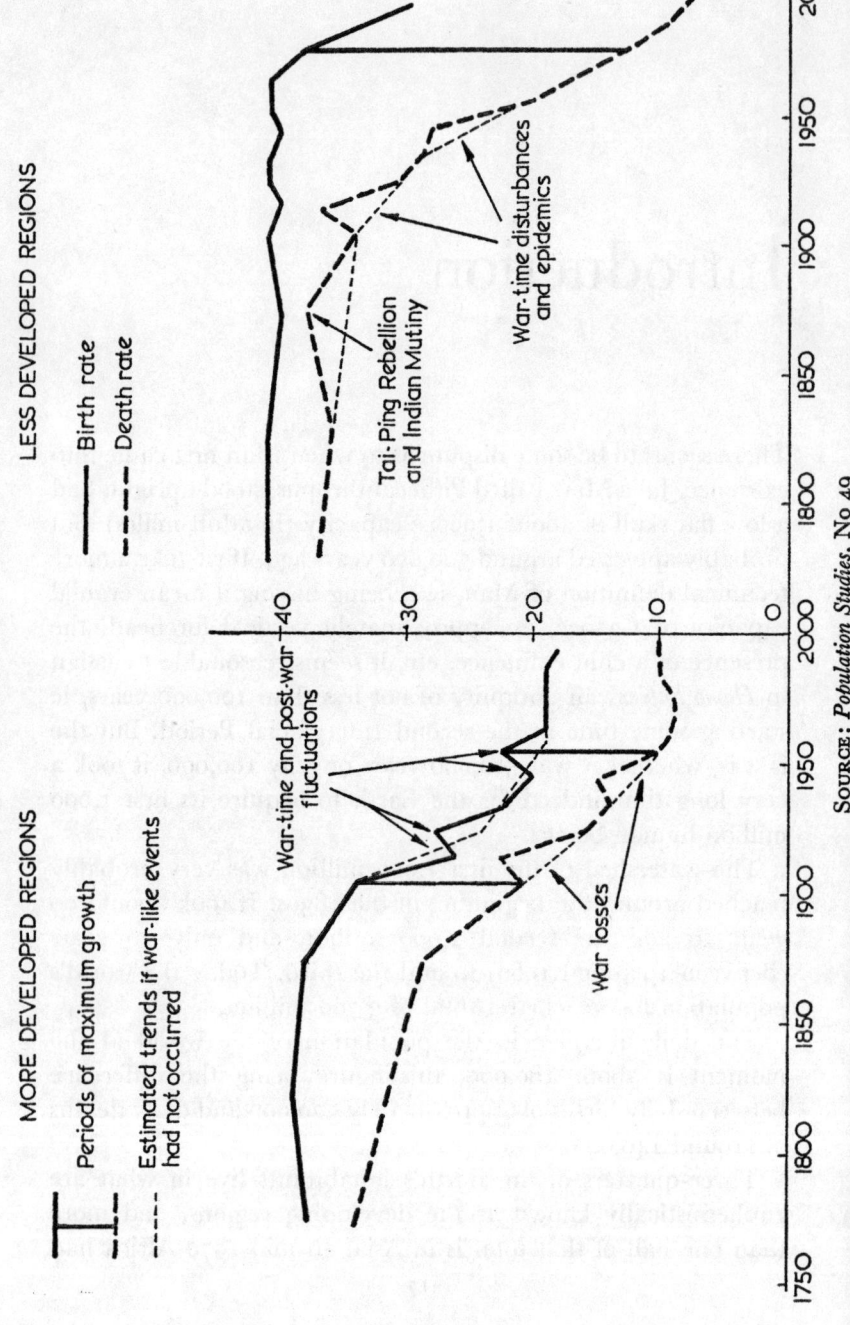

Fig 1 Estimated and conjectured trends in birth and death rates, 1750–2000

SOURCE: *Population Studies*, No 49

344 million, North America 228 million, Latin America 283 million, Asia 2,056 million, Europe 462 million, and Oceania 19·4 million. The population of mainland China, incidentally, was estimated at 765 million.

The percentage annual rate of population increase between 1963 and 1968 was 2·4 in Africa, 2 in Asia, 0·8 in Europe, 2·9 in Latin America, 1·3 in North America, 2 in Oceania and 1·1 in the Soviet Union. The highest figure—3·5 per cent—is reported for Central America, where the birth rate is 45 per 1,000 population, while the death rate has been reduced to 11 per 1,000. Female babies in Iceland have the longest expectation of life (76·2 years). For male babies, the longest life expectancy is in Sweden (71·6 years).

Women in Jordan and Bahrain have the world's highest fertility rate and produce, on the average, five children each. For the world as a whole there are each year 33 live births per 1,000 people and around 14 deaths per 1,000 people. World population growth is entirely the result of natural increase—the excess of births over deaths, which for the world is now 19 per 1,000. But whereas during Man's history there have been many fluctuations of population, this latest extreme and unprecedented growth—even 'explosion'—of population is the result of a decline of mortality over the last two centuries which has produced a divergence of the birth and death rates and hence a much increased rate of natural increase (see Fig 1). The very successes we have had in raising standards of living and in extending health services have produced the most serious consequences.

When death rates began to fall as they did in Europe in the nineteenth century (see Table 1), more and more children survived to adulthood and were themselves able to produce children. The rate of natural increase of the now more developed world grew from a level of about 4 per 1,000 before 1800 to 10 per 1,000. During the last century (1850–1950) birth rates in the more developed world have been halved and now, after the postwar boom of the 1950s, natural increase rates seem to be declining; but they are not expected throughout the developed regions to fall below 8 per 1,000 before the turn of the century.

TABLE I

Estimated and conjectured average annual birth rates, death rates and rates of natural increase for currently more developed and less developed regions, 1960–70, and selected periods, 1750–2000

Period	More developed regions*			Less developed regions		
	Birth rate	Death rate	Natural increase	Birth rate	Death rate	Natural increase
	(per 1,000 per year)			(per 1,000 per year)		
1960–70	20	9	11	41	17	24
Half centuries						
1750–1850	38	34	4	41	37	4
1800–50	39	32	7	41	36	5
1850–1900	38	29	9	40	38	2
1900–50	26	18	8	41	32	9
1950–2000	20	10	10	37	14	23

* More developed regions—Europe, USSR, USA, Canada, Japan, Temperate South America, Australia, New Zealand.

SOURCE: *Population Studies*, No 49

The great reductions in mortality did not reach the two-thirds of mankind in the developing nations of Asia, Latin America and Africa until after World War II. Since the death rate is now falling fast while the birth rate remains high, these areas are experiencing rates of natural increase on a scale not experienced by the now more developed countries. Latin America is the most rapidly growing continental region at almost 30 per 1,000 a year. It is followed by South Asia at almost 28 per 1,000 and Africa at over 25 per 1,000.

The difference between birth rate and death rate produces distinct distributions of population according to age from region to region. If we divide the nations among categories of population growth, we find that Asia and Africa are in the high-fertility with high-mortality categories, while three-fifths of

Latin America come under high fertility and moderate mortality. Europe and Japan at the other end of the scale have low fertility and low mortality. In these more developed countries the death rate is unlikely to fall, because of the population structure, and so any further reduction in fertility produces an immediate effect on natural increase rates. In contrast, in less developed countries birth rates would have to be very sharply reduced to make any impact on natural increase against a still falling death rate and the high potential fertility of the many children.

The United Nations Population Division from time to time produce projections of what the world population would be under different assumptions of fertility and mortality. (The effect of migration, of course, has no worldwide significance and little regionally.) The point about these UN calculations is that they are *projections*, not forecasts. They say what *would* happen if the assumption proved correct. They do not say what *will* happen.

On the assumption that the world's present fertility rates remain unchanged but continued modest declines in mortality are experienced, we would end up in the year 2000 with a world of about 8,000 million people.

A continuation of population growth at the present rate would be disastrous for the developing world. Increases of 2·5 per cent or 3 per cent per annum may not sound very much to most of us, who have to pay 9 per cent on our mortgages, but compounded year by year, day by day, hour by hour, it adds up. Pakistan's population, at its present growth rate, will double in 21 years, India's in 27, Ghana's in 24, Algeria's in 21, the Yemen's in 25, Brazil's in 25.

At the most basic level, it is still a question of people versus food. The FAO index of all farm products rose from 74 in 1934–8 to 148 in 1970 while the UN population index rose only from 83 to 134 in the same time.

These increases in agricultural production give room for hope that governments, temporarily reprieved from the threat of

Malthusian catastrophes, may have the time to find humane solutions to their problems. But many qualifications need to be made even to this cautious statement. Agronomists are keenly aware of the need for proper husbandry of the new strains of wheat and rice, of the importance of the right application and combination of inputs, of the need for credit and marketing facilities. Many financial and administrative constraints will have to be eliminated before yield increases, which have been achieved over a short time span in certain parts of the developing world, can be sustained, and improved upon, over a wider area. Only continued research can tell what further increases in agricultural production can be expected; only experience can show the dimensions of the political and social problems which will undoubtedly be caused by the 'green revolution'.

Food is, of course, only one aspect—though a vital aspect—of the population/resource equation. The satisfaction of other needs implies far more than a full bowl of rice.

In low income countries where the size of the population is doubling every 25 years or less, for instance, almost intolerable burdens are placed on the educational system. When the proportion of the society under 15 years of age is over 40 per cent, and rising, the absolute number of illiterates is likely to increase rather than diminish, however many schools are built and teachers trained. The strains thrown on the fragile structure of public health facilities may be of similar magnitude.

Or again, the relentless increase in population in rural areas, taken in conjunction with existing underemployment in agriculture, may accentuate the pressures of rural/urban migration. In the cities, inability to invest in sufficient new jobs, combined with the capital intensive bias of industrial technology and the natural increase of urban populations themselves, may lead to the most massive problems of unemployment, squalor and unrest—threatening the very foundations of public order.

In aggregate terms the rate of population growth in the developing world renders difficult, if not impossible of attainment, rapid increases in *per capita* income. For example, with a

GNP which is growing at an annual rate of 5 per cent and a stationary population it takes 12 years to double *per capita* income. If population growth is rising, say, at 2·4 per cent a year (the projected average rate for the less developed world), it will take 27 years to achieve a doubling in *per capita* income. If the annual growth in national income is 4 per cent rather than 5 per cent, doubling of *per capita* income will take 43 years; and since two-thirds of the population live in countries where *per capita* income is less than $300 per annum and often less than $100, even twice the present income is hardly likely to represent a satisfactory fulfilment of economic expectation.

What can be done about the population explosion in the developing countries?

The first thing to make clear is that the only people who can do anything about the population problems of the developing countries are the people of those countries themselves. If there was any underlying theme in the International Development Strategy for the second United Nations development decade, adopted by the General Assembly in October 1970, it was that the primary responsibility for the development of the developing countries rests on themselves. This is as true of population as of any other field of activity.

In fact, in this matter of population, there has been very considerable progress over the last few years. The Population Division of the United Nations keeps a running score of governments with official population policies and the total now is over twenty. They include India, mainland China, Pakistan, Indonesia, the Philippines, Thailand, Iran, the UAR, Ghana, Taiwan, Turkey, South Korea, Morocco, Kenya, Malaysia, Ceylon, Nepal, the Dominican Republic, Tunisia, Mauritius, Singapore and Jamaica. Other governments provide assistance for family planning without having an official population policy. These include Nigeria, Colombia, Venezuela, Costa Rica, Ecuador, El Salvador, Honduras, Panama, Nicaragua, Dahomey, Hong Kong, Chile and Botswana.

Family planning must be a familiar enough term to the Western audience. In an organised institutionalised way Britain virtually invented the idea. The essential philosophy is that a married couple (or indeed any other kind of couple) should have the number of children they want and no more. So as not to have *more* children than they want, the husband or wife (or possibly both) practise some form of contraception. The methods, which there is no need to go into here, are familiar. Family planners tend to advocate what they call the 'cafeteria' approach: anything will do as long as it works, from abstinence at one end of the spectrum to the latest hormonal preparations and vasectomy at the other.

The bulk of the effort in the developing countries has so far been concentrated in the extension of family planning programmes. National Family Planning Associations, affiliated to the International Planned Parenthood Federation (IPPF), see p 202) work in seventy-nine countries. Where governments have official family planning programmes, either inside or outside the health service, the Family Planning Association will work alongside and try to dovetail its efforts into the government's own programme. Where governments do not yet have family planning programmes, the private Family Planning Association can bring pressure and influence to bear and can hope to demonstrate to the government that family planning is something women want and governments should provide.

Now it is conceivable that if family planning services, ie organised contraception, was widely and cheaply available, so that all couples had as many children as they wanted and no more, then we might arrive at a rate of population growth that was acceptable and tolerable and did not impose excessive burdens on the economy and social structure of the country or on the environment. But the trouble is, all over the world, people tend to want *too many* children from a demographic point of view. There is, of course, endless speculation as to why this is so. Some argue that the collective consciousness in developing countries has not yet woken up to the fact that more babies are surviving than used to and that it is no longer necessary to have, say, seven children in order to have a net gain of two.

Others point to deeply ingrained patterns of behaviour: children are needed to revere dead ancestors, the more the better; two sons at least may be required to open up the father's skull on the funeral pyre; children may provide support and succour to their parents in countries where the social security system is virtually non-existent; agricultural systems in much of the developing world require a ready availability of labour at certain times of the year, even if there is a good deal of unemployment or underemployment at other times. Consequently the probability of a population policy being successfully implemented solely through the provision of family planning services—*as a non-priority matter*—is remote. This is not to say that there may not be important additions to human welfare from family planning programmes. No doubt, from the point of view of the individual mother and family, the provision of family planning can be seen as a boon and a relief from the burden of constant childbearing. But it will not bring the birth rate down, or not very much.

That is why countries like India or Pakistan and Indonesia and the UAR which, on broad socio-economic grounds, so desperately *do* need to bring their birth rates down, ie those countries which have official population policies and defined demographic goals, have decided to do more than merely provide family planning services. They have decided to publicise them and to propagandise.

The idea is that the state has at its disposal an arsenal of devices to influence people's desires and inclinations. The word often used to describe this process is 'motivation'. The instruments of motivation may be human—the family planning worker wobbling her way on a bicycle through the villages of Taiwan bringing the good news—or they may be mechanical, like movies and mass address systems, television programmes and huge billboards posted in the streets. Or again, the instruments of motivation may have to do with incentives and disincentives, privileges and penalties.

There is admittedly not much evidence (except in the case of mainland China) that this wider approach is working. There have been limited successes in achieving modest reductions in the birth rate in countries like Taiwan, Singapore, Hong Kong and Korea, but it is not clear what relation there is between these successes and the deliberate implementation by the state of population policies.

There are those who argue that a falling birth rate is a consequence of a general rise in the level of economic and social development. They continue the argument by saying that, so far from investing large sums of money in population programmes that will have no effect, since you *cannot* change from the outside people's fundamental attitudes to something as important and intimate as procreation, you should put this money into 'conventional' development programmes. The standard of living rose in the West, they say, and that itself induced a decline in fertility. When people *wanted* to have fewer children, they found a way. This is known as 'the theory of demographic transition'. The idea is that after a certain period of time another category can be added to the ones mentioned earlier. After falling fertility and low mortality, you reach low fertility and low mortality.

There is evidence that what happened in the West will be repeated in some developing countries. The peripheral areas and Asia mentioned above have come within the orbit of the Western Industrial System and Japan has seen a very remarkable check in population growth with its development as a major industrial nation. The signs of a slower rate of growth in China are of great consequence. UN projections for East Asia (without Japan) and for middle South Asia (India and Pakistan) give the slowest rates of growth for all the less developed regions, and a fall to 13 per 100 and 22 per 1,000 per annum respectively by the end of the century. These two regions together have half the world's population, and population trends here are crucial for the future of mankind. But from a glance at the population growth figures for most of the less developed world, the idea of demographic transition seems a chicken and ovum proposition. Until and unless population growth rates can be brought down—and, after all, the effort is very recent indeed, so we should not be discouraged by the lack of progress so far—it is hard to see how there can be enough investment resources available in most developing countries to finance modernisation and, to paraphrase Walt Rostow, to ensure a 'take-off into self-sustaining fertility decline'.

So what do we do? Do we wait, as Lord Snow so vividly put it, for the starving millions to die on the television screens in our living-rooms? Or are there some practical steps we can take?

Yes, there are practical steps. The encouraging thing is that Western governments are giving more and more vigorous support to developing countries. This support, aimed at ensuring that a high priority is given to population and family planning programmes, is being principally channelled through international agencies.

The past 25 years have, in fact, seen the United Nations and its system of agencies increasingly involved in this field. The early work of the United Nations' Population Division did much to establish the nature and extent of the problem, at least as far as the broad demographic projections are concerned. The Specialised Agencies gradually came to a clearer understanding of the implications of population increase in their own fields—health, agriculture, employment and education.

By the middle of the first UN Development Decade (1965), an intense debate was under way in the UN itself and in other international forums, such as the World Health Assembly, the Executive Board of UNICEF, etc, as to whether the population question was one the UN system should properly be concerned with—*in an operational sense*. Was there any mandate, for example, for UN action in the field of family planning.

This question proved to be one of the most controversial the organisation had ever faced—at least in the economic and social sphere. The plea for UN action came from countries like India and Pakistan, which, convinced of the immensity of their own 'population problems', were anxious to have help wherever they could find it, especially through 'multilateral' channels (supposedly) free of any racial or political bias. Support for the Indian position was forthcoming from the Scandinavian countries and, especially, from the United States. Once President Eisenhower had reversed his earlier opposition to US Government involvement in family planning programmes at home or abroad, the United States placed increasing emphasis on the urgency of the population problem. This emphasis was continued and intensified during the administration of John F. Kennedy, the first Catholic President.

The opposition to United Nations action came primarily from the following: Catholic countries of Europe, such as Belgium, Ireland and Italy; Catholic countries of Latin America, like Brazil and Mexico, which, anyway, did not believe they had a population problem and suspected the heavy hand of Yankee imperialism in this, as in so many other fields; and some newly emerged and racially sensitive African countries, which felt themselves to be underpopulated, and, at least in the case of French-speaking Africa, subject to restrictive French laws concerning birth control. France has itself had a recent history of population decline, and, religious issues aside, is now actively promoting population growth. In the USSR and most of the Eastern European bloc, which had severe labour shortages after World War II and where declining populations since have aggravated the problem, particularly in Hungary and Czechoslovakia, official policies of population growth are reinforced by 'ideological themes'. Others, though not necessarily falling into any of the previous categories, have felt that the United Nations was in danger of paying too much attention to fertility, to the exclusion of more important questions.

Nevertheless, by 1966, what became known as a historic 'breakthrough' had occurred. The General Assembly adopted a broad resolution authorising the United Nations to give assistance when required in the field of population and family planning. In due course the Specialised Agencies evolved their own parallel mandates. Even the WHO, in which the debate had been most bitter, began by deliberately stressing the health aspects of family planning. The United Nations Commissions on Human Rights, on the Status of Women and on Social Development took up similar positions. The promotion of family planning as a 'human right'—an approach vigorously advocated by organisations like the International Planned Parenthood Federation (IPPF)—seemed to avoid some of the political pitfalls.

By 1967 the Secretary-General of the United Nations had established a Trust Fund for Population. Throughout 1967 and 1968 contributions to the fund remained low (around $1·5 million) because the key question had not been resolved. Where was the fund to be located and how was it to be administered? In effect, the disposition of the fund became an important item in the larger debate which was then going on—and which still continues—concerning the relative roles of the UN Development Programme (UNDP) and the rest of the system.

In the event the Administrator of UNDP (then Paul Hoffman) was asked to handle the Population Fund. In late 1969 Mr Hoffman appointed Rafael Salas, previously Executive Secretary of the Philippines, as the fund's first Executive Director. As a Catholic from the Third World, Salas could be seen as an inspired choice.

The last 2 years have witnessed a rapid growth in the Population Fund's resources and responsibilities. Its budget has risen from $1·5 million in 1969 to over $40 million in 1972. An important change in the fund's programming is the movement away from small projects handled regionally and interregionally towards more comprehensive country projects, such as those that are now being supported in India, Indonesia, Iran, the Philippines, Thailand and the UAR.

Besides the IPPF and the UNFPA, there is the World Bank. There is no doubt that Mr McNamara's forthright recognition that without parallel efforts at population control the value of much development assistance would be vitiated has been of fundamental importance in moving the bank in this new direction. The bank now has a Population Projects Department and has already made several loans or grants for population projects. At the moment it is contemplating further grants to a variety of countries. The word 'grants' is used advisedly. However persuasive cost-benefit economists may be in identifying the 'rate of return' on investment in family planning, most governments are still unwilling to accept 'hard', ie interest-bearing repayable, money for this purpose. They prefer grants or credit. But this attitude may change in time, if and when demographers are able to demonstrate that all these efforts do indeed have an effect, and that through the implementation of population and family planning programmes a sustained decline in fertility can be achieved.

Perhaps the most appropriate note to strike is one of 'guarded optimism'. There have indeed been great developments in the last few years. Much has been achieved at least in building up the 'institutional infrastructure' through which the war on population growth is to be waged.

The war is by no means won, however. The initial success of UNFPA has to some extent obscured a 'population backlash' which has—especially since the Encyclical *Humanae Vitae*—been gathering momentum. The opposition to UN involvement in population and family planning programmes did not disappear in 1966 when the General Assembly adopted its enabling resolution. It merely withdrew so as to regroup. The next months and years will show how strong and how effective it remains. The position of the Vatican will be of special interest.

We are now witnessing another shift in the focus of the population debate: throughout the 1960s the population problem was largely thought of as being a matter of concern to the developing countries, but today it is more and more being presented as relevant to *all* countries. Though the Stockholm UN Conference on the Environment in June 1972 failed to deal with the topic in any depth, the relations between population growth and distribution and environmental deterioration are receiving a good deal of attention.

Daily the evidence is accumulating that the population issue is just as relevant to the fat rich white countries of the world as it is to the thin poor coloured countries. Daily there is wider recognition of the fact that it is not just a question of the rate of population growth, but of population growth multiplied by affluence and the force of technology itself. The United States, for instance, with 6 per cent of the world's population, in 1966 consumed 34 per cent of the world's energy production. In 1968 some 1,660 million people living in the developing countries together used 25 per cent less energy than did the 185 million people living in the six countries of the European Community.

The advanced nations, much more than the poorer nations, are squandering the resources of Spaceship Earth. There may be some doubt about the precise value of the population coefficient in the population/affluence/technology product, but one thing is certain—the more people there are, the more pollution, environmental degradation and resource depletion there will be.

The population problem in Britain has, too, to be seen in an international as well as a national perspective. With the other EEC countries we support international agencies specialising in population control overseas, but the European rate of natural increase of 8 per 1,000 is still double the level that existed before the population surge of the last two centuries. Within the EEC, moreover, some countries, like France, are lukewarm in their support of birth control.

How much of the population-environment message comes across in schools and universities? What is the state of teaching regarding, say, ecology, environment, birth control and, more generally, 'population-awareness', to use a term which is becoming fashionable in United Nations jargon? How adequate are present geography and other curricula and educational concepts? How ambitious can a teacher be in, say, the Gorbals of Glasgow in putting across large ecological concerns about respect for nature? What kind of priority can be given to urging on children, who may themselves come from large families, the morality of the small family norm?

A good deal of thought is now being given in UNESCO and elsewhere to the nature of population education. Definitions are being established and strategies worked out. Money is available largely through the United Nations Fund for Population Activities, for propaganda on a massive scale. The hope is that, from a reproductive point of view, the next generation may be persuaded to behave more responsibly than the last.

But population and reproduction are only part of the story, and, in the nature of things, it is easier for organisations like UNESCO to find money for programmes in Lusaka and Bombay than in London and Tokyo. We must look to our own laurels, do our own research, teach the teachers so that they in turn can teach the children. All this is a matter of urgency. The post-industrial society will not be born overnight.

This book is an attempt to bring together some of the main facts about the population explosion, some documentary material relating to it, and information about men and institutions involved in attempts to 'solve' the population problem. It has been published at this time because of the imminence—in 1974—of World Population Year and of the first ever World Conference of governments on population and what to do about it. Unlike the previous World Population Conferences (held in Rome in 1954 and Belgrade in 1965), this will be an official governmental (as opposed to scientific) conference. The United Nations is fortunate in having found a distinguished former Mexican foreign minister, Don Antonio Carrillo-Flores, to take charge of the preparations.

What will the World Population Conference achieve? Work is at present proceeding on the draft of a World Population Plan of Action to be discussed at the conference. Conceivably this document will be approved by a majority of delegates as a basis for subsequent programmes. Conceivably the conference will take steps to strengthen the central role of the Population Fund in working with other agencies of the United Nations system, especially the World Bank, and with key non-governmental organisations like IPPF (IPPF's Secretary-General, Dr Julia Henderson, is herself a former senior UN official); and, above all, in providing large-scale assistance direct to the countries themselves. Conceivably, the World Conference may even agree on worldwide or regional targets for reduction in the rate of population growth. The hope is that the nations may come together and collectively agree to limit the insane proliferation of the human species, wherever it occurs.

Even if worldwide goals of population stability are proclaimed and adopted, however, it will be a long and weary struggle to achieve them. According to Dr Berelson, President of the Population Council, assuming it was possible for the world's peoples to attain a reproduction rate of only two children per couple (a net reproduction rate of unity) by any date in the reasonably near future, the population would continue to grow for an additional 65–70 years and the ultimate stabilised level would be far greater than at the time the two per couple rate was achieved. If, for example, the net reproduction rate of unity was achieved by the turn of the century (an extremely unlikely assumption), the world's population would not stabilise until the end of the next century, at over 8,000 million people. If a net reproduction rate of unity was not achieved until the year 2040, worldwide population would not stabilise until around 2120 at 14,500 million—owing to the legacy of past population growth on the age-structure of society and on the numbers of women entering childbearing age.

Only those who believe that the universe and its resources are infinite or, alternatively, have an infinite capacity for self-delusion can deny the necessity of each and every nation, sooner or later, adopting a population policy. And, if it has to come sooner or later, then why not sooner? The task itself is difficult enough and progress, even under the most favourable conditions, will be slow.

PART ONE

Facts and Figures and Their Meaning

FERTILITY AND POPULATION GROWTH

As we have said, it took from the beginning of man to about 1830 AD *for the earth's population to reach its first 1,000 million inhabitants, another 100 years to add the second 1,000 million and 30 years (between 1930 and 1960) to add the third. Sometime in 1974, the 4,000 million mark will be passed.*

If we assume a continuation of present levels of fertility, the world's population would reach about 8,000 million, or more than double its present total, by the end of the century; 6,000 million (or three-quarters of these people) would live in the developing countries. Even with declines in fertility, the world's population may reach 4,457 million in 1980, 5,438 million in 1990 and 6,494 million by the end of the century. In this event the population of the less developed regions would total 5,040 million in the year 2000.

1 UN
YOUTHFULNESS OF WORLD POPULATION

In the more developed regions, 28 per cent of the population were children and youth below 15 years of age in 1965, and that percentage may fall to 26 by 1985; persons aged 65 years and more constituted 9 per cent in 1965 and may amount to 10 per cent in 1985; consequently the segment in the most productive ages, between 15 and 64 years, may remain in the neighbourhood of 63 per cent of the total. In the less developed regions, owing to their higher fertility, 42 per cent of the population were aged under 15 years in 1965, and 3 per cent were 65 years and older, hence 55 per cent were in the ages between 15 and 64; by 1985, the proportion aged under 15 may have diminished to 40 per cent, those 65 years and over may have increased to 4 per cent, and the proportion in ages from 15 to 64 may then amount to 56 per cent.

These differences in age structure, especially between the more developed and less developed regions, have important implications for priorities in economic and social investment.
SOURCE: UN. *A Concise Summary of the World Population Situation in 1970*

Fig 2 shows the growth and distribution of population under the 'constant fertility' assumption. The dominant role of Asia (including India and China) is obvious.

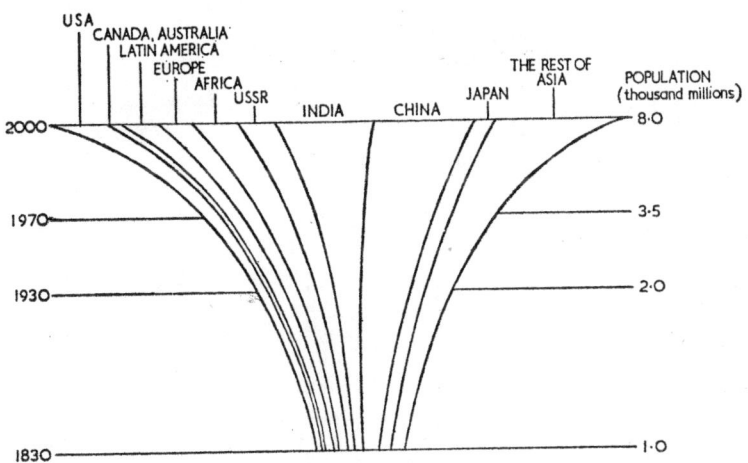

Fig 2 Distribution of population, 1830–2000

SOURCE: United Nations Association of the United States of America: *World Population—a report of a National Policy Panel*

Fig 3 shows the births throughout the world in 1970 divided by percentage among regions.

Fig 3 World births in percentages by region, 1970

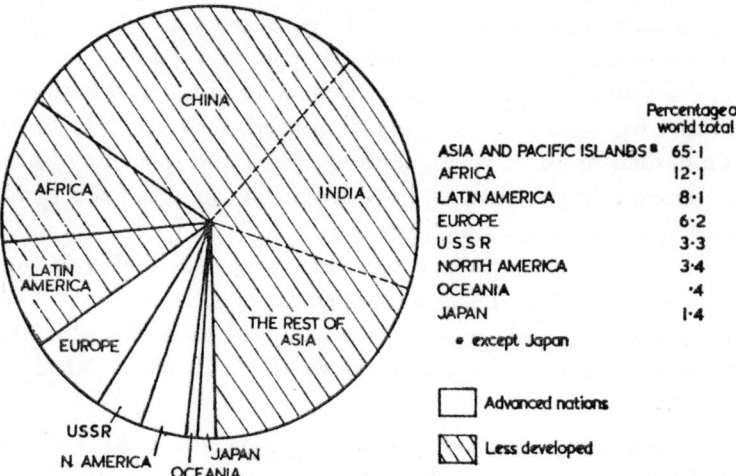

SOURCE: Estimates of International Demographic Statistical Center, Census Bureau, supplied by USAID

TABLE 2
World population increase, 1965–70

	Annual per cent increase		Annual absolute increase (millions)	
	1960–5	1965–70	1960–5	1965–70
World total	1·94	1·98	61·1	68·2
More developed regions	1·15	0·95	11·5	10·0
Less developed regions	2·32	2·45	49·6	58·2
East Asia	1·75	1·75	14·4	15·5
South Asia	2·48	2·75	23·1	28·6
Europe	0·84	0·78	3·7	3·4
Soviet Union	1·52	1·02	3·4	2·4
Africa	2·41	2·55	7·0	8·3
Northern America	1·34	0·98	2·7	2·2
Latin America	2·82	2·84	6·6	7·6
Oceania	1·69	1·45	0·2	0·2

SOURCE: *UN Demographic Yearbook 1970*

Table 2 shows the world population between 1960 and 1970. It can be seen that by the end of the period the world total was increasing at almost 2 per cent a year, which meant a net addition of almost 70 million persons each year, 58 million of them in the less developed regions. Table 3 shows world population in 1970.

POPULATION PROJECTIONS

The World Leaders' Statement (see p 174) says there will be 'nearly seven billion' people on this earth in the year 2,000 at 'today's rate of increase'. In fact since 1967 the rate of increase has itself accelerated. The United Nations has revised its projections upwards. In making these projections the UN uses four different variants: the 'constant fertility' variant assumes that the population of the less developed regions will maintain 1965 levels of fertility; the 'high', 'medium' and 'low' variants all assume that the gross reproduction rate in the less developed countries will decrease by 5 per cent during the first 5 year period, by 10 per cent within each of the next two 5 year periods and by 15 per cent during each of the next 5 year periods, so that within 30 years the gross reproduction rate would be about half its initial value. What distinguishes the 'high', 'medium' and 'low' variants from each other is the assumption made with regard to the date this pattern of fertility decline begins. The 'low' variant makes the assumption that the onset of fertility decline began in 1970 (though this, of course, can already be shown to be a false assumption; thus projections based on the 'low' variant will be too low). The 'medium' variant assumes a starting date of 1975 and the 'high' variant a starting date of 1980.

What grounds are there to suppose that the general pattern of fertility decline, as assumed in the 'high', 'medium' and 'low' variants will be achieved (leaving aside the question of the specific starting date)? This is a complex matter but the broad answer seems to lie in assuming (i) that the general level of development in less developed countries will exert an effect on fertility, and (ii) that the existence of population and family planning policies and their implementation will also affect fertility.

Thus the difference between the total of 6,369 million inhabitants in the developing countries under the 'constant fertility' assumption and

TABLE 3
World population, 1970 (mid-year estimates)

	Population (in millions)	Rate of increase (per cent)	Birth rate (per thousand)	Death rate (per thousand)
World	3,633	2·0	34	14
Africa	344	2·6	46	20
Western Africa	101	2·5	49	24
Eastern Africa	98	2·5	43	18
Northern Africa	87	3·1	48	17
Middle Africa	36	2·1	45	24
Southern Africa	23	2·4	41	17
America	511	2·1	30	10
North America	228	1·2	18	9
Latin America	283	2·9	39	10
Tropical S. America	151	3·0	41	11
Middle America	67	3·4	44	10
Temperate S. America	39	1·8	26	8
Caribbean	26	2·3	36	13
Asia	2,056	2·3	38	15
Eastern Asia	930	1·8	31	13
Mainland	765	1·8	33	15
Japan	103	1·1	18	7
Other Eastern Asia	61	2·5	34	9
South Asia	1,126	2·8	44	16
Middle S. Asia	762	2·8	45	17
S.E. Asia	287	2·8	43	15
S.W. Asia	77	2·9	43	14
Europe	462	0·8	18	10
Western Europe	149	0·8	17	11
Southern Europe	128	0·9	19	9
Eastern Europe	104	0·8	17	10
North eastern Europe	81	0·6	18	11
Oceania	19·4	2·0	24	10
Australia and New Zealand	15·4	1·9	20	9
Melanesia	2·8	2·4	42	18
Polynesia and Micronesia	1·2	3·1	40	9
USSR	242	1·0	18	8

SOURCE: *UN Demographic Yearbook 1970*

4,523 under the 'low' assumption—a difference of almost 2000 million—can be seen as a kind of target figure. If we go on the way we are going, we would have an 8,000 million world in the year 2,000, because to the 6,400 million inhabitants of the LDCs must be added 1,500 million inhabitants of developed countries (where a single 'medium' variant is assumed). If, on the other hand, development and population policies are successful, we might be able to 'lop off' 2,000 million from this figure and achieve a population of 6,000 million in the year 2000, with all the benefits this would bring for current and future generations.

Tables 4–7 and the commentary were prepared by the Population Division of the United Nations.

2 UN Population Division
COMMENTS ON TOTAL POPULATION GROWTH

Tables 4–7 present the results of total population estimates and annual rates of growth by regions during the period 1965–2000, according to the above mentioned four variants. The world population of 3,289 million in 1965 is expected, according to the 'medium' variant, to increase to 6,494 million in 2000. The implied rates of growth indicate that the world population may be growing at almost a constant rate of about 2·0 per cent annually until the middle of the 1980s, and then the rate would gradually decrease until it reaches 1·7 per cent by the end of the century. During the period under consideration, the population of the less developed regions is anticipated to increase from 2,252 million to 5,040 million, with a rate of growth which would remain virtually constant and equal to about 2·4 until 1985 and then gradually decrease to 2·0 per cent per annum. On the other hand, the population of the more developed regions may sustain an almost constant annual rate of about 1·0 per cent throughout the remainder of this century, thus increasing from 1,037 million in 1965 to 1,454 million at the turn of the century. As a result of these differing rates of growth, the projected population of the less developed regions is expected to be about three and a half times the projected figure for the developed regions at the end of the century, while the ratio in 1965 was only a little over two to one.

According to the 'low' and 'high' variants, the range within which the population of the less developed countries would probably fall by the end of the century is from 4,523 to 5,650 million. The 'high' variant implies an acceleration of population growth at a rate equal to 2·6 or 2·7 per cent per annum until 1985 followed by a gradual decline in the rate of growth to 2·4 per cent per annum during 1995–2000. The 'low' variant envisages a more moderate rate of population growth which would gradually decrease from 2·3 to 1·6 by the end of the century (Tables 5–6). In the 'constant fertility' variant, the rates of growth given in Table 7 indicate that if the population of the less developed regions maintain their 1965 levels of fertility they would have an accelerated increase in their annual rates of growth, from 2·6 in 1965–70 to probably 3·4 in 1995–2000, and their total population may reach 6,369 million by the end of the century.

Among the world's major areas the largest addition to the population during the 35-year projection period is expected in South Asia, which contains almost one-third of the world's population. As the data in Tables 4–7 show, the population of this major area is anticipated to increase from 981 million to 2,354 million in the year 2000 according to the 'medium' variant, and it may still reach to 2,617 million if the assumptions of the 'high' variant materialize. The next major area of importance with respect to addition of population numbers, according to the 'medium' variant, is East Asia where, although the pace of growth is expected to be moderate (from 1·8 in the beginning of the projection period to 1·1 in the end), the absolute increase will be very high. Sizeable increases in total population are also expected in Latin America, from 246 million in 1965 to 652 million in 2000, and in Africa, from 303 million to 818 million during the same period. It is also to be noted that for the year 2000 the 'constant fertility' estimate of total population is higher than the 'medium' estimate by 27 per cent in

TABLE 4

Total population estimates and annual rates of growth by regions, 1965–2000
Medium variant

Regions	Total population (in thousands)					Annual rates of growth (per cent)			
	1965	1970	1980	1990	2000	1965–70	1970–5	1980–5	1990–5	1995–2000
World total	3,289,002	3,631,797	4,456,688	5,438,169	6,493,642	2·0	2·0	2·0	1·8	1·7
More developed regions	1,037,492	1,090,297	1,210,051	1,336,499	1,453,528	1·0	1·0	1·0	0·9	0·8
Less developed regions	2,251,510	2,541,501	3,246,637	4,101,670	5,040,114	2·4	2·5	2·4	2·1	2·0
East Asia	851,877	929,932	1,095,354	1,265,343	1,424,377	1·8	1·7	1·5	1·2	1·1
Mainland Region	700,076	765,386	901,351	1,042,864	1,176,176	1·8	1·7	1·5	1·3	1·1
Japan	97,950	103,499	116,347	125,330	132,760	1·1	1·2	0·8	0·6	0·6
Other East Asia	53,851	61,046	77,656	97,148	115,442	2·5	2·4	2·4	1·8	1·6
South Asia	981,046	1,125,843	1,485,714	1,911,819	2,353,841	2·8	2·8	2·6	2·2	2·0
Middle South Asia	664,868	761,809	1,001,046	1,279,761	1,564,963	2·7	2·8	2·5	2·1	1·9
South East Asia	249,349	286,925	380,367	491,775	607,709	2·8	2·9	2·7	2·2	2·0
South West Asia	66,829	77,109	104,302	140,283	181,169	2·9	3·0	3·0	2·7	2·4
Europe	444,642	462,120	497,061	532,636	568,358	0·8	0·7	0·7	0·7	0·6
Western Europe	143,143	148,619	158,214	168,679	179,266	0·8	0·6	0·6	0·6	0·6
Southern Europe	122,750	128,466	140,059	151,605	162,674	0·9	0·9	0·8	0·7	0·7
Eastern Europe	100,060	104,082	112,392	119,607	127,277	0·8	0·8	0·7	0·7	0·6
Northern Europe	78,689	80,953	86,396	92,745	99,141	0·6	0·6	0·7	0·7	0·7

Regions	Total population (in thousands)					Annual rates of growth (per cent)			
	1965	1970	1980	1990	2000	1965–70	1970–5	1980–5	1990–5	1995–2000
USSR	230,556	242,612	270,634	302,011	329,508	1·0	1·0	1·2	0·9	0·8
Africa	303,150	344,484	456,721	615,826	817,751	2·6	2·8	3·0	2·9	2·8
Western Africa	89,546	101,272	133,406	180,059	240,158	2·5	2·7	3·0	3·0	2·8
Eastern Africa	86,448	97,882	128,757	173,639	233,245	2·5	2·7	2·9	3·0	2·9
Middle Africa	32,318	35,893	45,785	60,449	80,214	2·1	2·4	2·7	2·9	2·8
Northern Africa	74,520	86,606	119,385	163,230	214,404	3·0	3·2	3·2	2·9	2·6
Southern Africa	20,318	22,832	29,387	38,450	49,730	2·3	2·5	2·7	2·6	2·5
Northern America	214,329	227,572	260,651	299,133	333,435	1·2	1·3	1·5	1·1	1·0
Latin America	245,884	283,253	377,172	499,771	652,337	2·8	2·9	2·8	2·7	2·6
Tropical South America	129,854	150,660	203,591	272,495	358,447	3·0	3·0	2·9	2·8	2·7
Middle America (Mainland)	56,961	67,430	94,706	132,387	180,476	3·4	3·4	3·4	3·2	3·0
Temperate South America	36,000	39,378	46,731	54,783	63,266	1·8	1·7	1·6	1·5	1·4
Caribbean	23,068	25,785	32,145	40,107	50,148	2·2	2·2	2·2	2·2	2·2
Oceania	17,520	19,370	24,025	29,639	35,173	2·0	2·1	2·2	1·8	1·6
Australia and New Zealand	14,015	15,374	18,785	22,659	26,214	1·9	2·0	2·0	1·5	1·4
Melanesia	2,452	2,767	3,585	4,743	6,107	2·4	2·6	2·8	2·6	2·4
Polynesia and Micronesia	1,053	1,229	1,657	2,237	2,853	3·1	3·1	3·1	2·6	2·3

SOURCE: UN Population Division

TABLE 5

Total population estimates and annual rates of growth by regions, 1965–2000

High variant

Less developed regions only

	Total population (in thousands)					Annual rates of growth (per cent)			
	1965	1970	1980	1990	2000	1965–70	1970–5	1980–5	1990–5	1995–2000
Less Developed Regions	2,251,510	2,563,561	3,378,768	4,424,950	5,650,426	2·6	2·7	2·7	2·5	2·4
Mainland Region	700,076	785,095	983,009	1,183,317	1,369,757	2·3	2·3	2·0	1·5	1·4
Other East Asia	53,851	61,046	78,845	102,115	123,424	2·5	2·5	2·7	2·1	1·7
South Asia	981,046	1,126,115	1,518,153	2,032,456	2,617,382	2·8	2·9	3·0	2·7	2·4
Middle South Asia	664,868	761,993	1,024,890	1,363,525	1,742,573	2·7	2·9	2·9	2·6	2·3
South East Asia	249,349	286,925	387,315	522,096	677,570	2·8	3·0	3·0	2·7	2·5
South West Asia	66,829	77,197	105,947	146,835	197,239	2·9	3·1	3·3	3·1	2·8
Africa	303,150	345,818	466,366	648,854	905,702	2·6	2·9	3·3	3·4	3·3
Western Africa	89,546	101,705	136,590	190,624	269,314	2·5	2·8	3·3	3·5	3·4
Eastern Africa	86,448	98,203	131,361	182,218	256,970	2·5	2·8	3·2	3·4	3·5
Middle Africa	32,318	36,013	46,754	63,457	88,626	2·2	2·5	3·0	3·3	3·4
Northern Africa	74,520	87,027	121,883	172,708	236,900	3·1	3·3	3·5	3·3	3·0
Southern Africa	20,318	22,871	29,778	39,847	53,892	2·4	2·6	2·8	3·0	3·0
Tropical South America	129,854	151,266	208,241	288,203	394,822	3·1	3·2	3·3	3·2	3·1
Middle America (Mainland)	56,961	67,498	96,505	138,609	196,659	3·4	3·5	3·7	3·5	3·5
Caribbean	23,068	25,851	32,754	41,915	53,842	2·3	2·3	2·5	2·5	2·5
Melanesia	2,452	2,771	3,645	4,963	6,625	2·4	2·6	3·0	3·0	2·8
Polynesia and Micronesia	1,053	1,230	1,737	2,472	3,337	3·1	3·4	3·6	3·1	2·9

SOURCE: UN Population Division

TABLE 6

Total population estimates and annual rates of growth by regions, 1965–2000

Low variant

Less developed regions only

	Total population (in thousands)					Annual rates of growth (per cent)				
	1965	1970	1980	1990	2000	1965–70	1970–5	1980–5	1990–5	1995–2000
Less Developed Regions	2,251,510	2,522,681	3,136,625	3,819,836	4,523,382	2·3	2·2	2·0	1·8	1·6
Mainland Region	700,076	752,802	855,508	945,776	1,034,638	1·5	1·4	1·0	0·9	0·9
Other East Asia	53,851	61,046	76,468	92,659	107,712	2·5	2·3	2·0	1·6	1·4
South Asia	981,046	1,121,456	1,438,771	1,785,862	2,119,009	2·7	2·6	2·3	1·8	1·6
Middle South Asia	664,868	758,481	967,173	1,191,467	1,403,391	2·6	2·5	2·2	1·7	1·6
South East Asia	249,349	286,062	369,499	461,531	550,240	2·7	2·6	2·4	1·9	1·7
South West Asia	66,829	76,914	102,100	132,864	165,378	2·8	2·8	2·7	2·3	2·1
Africa	303,150	343,596	448,006	582,872	734,159	2·5	2·6	2·7	2·4	2·2
Western Africa	89,546	100,928	130,536	168,751	210,587	2·4	2·5	2·6	2·3	2·1
Eastern Africa	86,448	97,637	126,633	165,633	211,152	2·4	2·6	2·7	2·5	2·3
Middle Africa	32,318	35,766	44,757	57,033	71,306	2·0	2·2	2·4	2·3	2·2
Northern Africa	74,520	86,470	116,964	154,130	194,285	3·0	3·1	2·8	2·4	2·2
Southern Africa	20,318	22,795	29,117	37,325	46,829	2·3	2·4	2·5	2·3	2·2
Tropical South America	129,854	150,035	198,648	257,832	325,152	2·9	2·8	2·7	2·4	2·2
Middle America (Mainland)	56,961	67,136	92,831	127,219	167,641	3·3	3·2	3·2	2·9	2·6
Caribbean	23,068	25,762	31,713	38,814	47,677	2·2	2·1	2·0	2·1	2·0
Melanesia	2,452	2,765	3,533	4,579	5,786	2·4	2·5	2·6	2·5	2·2
Polynesia and Micronesia	1,053	1,213	1,632	2,179	2,733	2·8	3·1	3·0	2·4	2·1

SOURCE: UN Population Division

TABLE 7

Total population estimates and annual rates of growth by regions, 1965–2000

Constant fertility variant

Less developed regions only

	Total population (in thousands)					Annual rates of growth (per cent)				
	1965	1970	1980	1990	2000	1965–70	1970–5	1980–5	1990–5	1995–2000
Less Developed Regions	2,251,510	2,559,001	3,381,131	4,583,220	6,368,737	2.6	2.7	3.0	3.2	3.4
Mainland Region	700,076	780,941	991,228	1,275,390	1,673,559	2.2	2.3	2.5	2.7	2.8
Other East Asia	53,851	61,573	82,445	113,879	156,700	2.7	2.8	3.2	3.2	3.2
South Asia	981,046	1,126,074	1,515,875	2,100,924	2,988,562	2.8	2.9	3.2	3.5	3.6
Middle South Asia	664,868	761,904	1,023,084	1,414,629	2,012,112	2.7	2.9	3.2	3.5	3.6
South East Asia	249,349	287,050	387,272	537,323	762,368	2.8	2.9	3.2	3.5	3.5
South West Asia	66,829	77,121	105,509	148,972	214,081	2.9	3.0	3.4	3.6	3.7
Africa	303,150	344,496	456,620	622,901	872,798	2.6	2.7	3.0	3.3	3.4
Western Africa	89,546	101,272	133,360	180,901	252,231	2.5	2.7	3.0	3.3	3.4
Eastern Africa	86,448	97,882	128,711	174,009	241,750	2.5	2.7	2.9	3.2	3.4
Middle Africa	32,318	35,958	45,603	59,449	79,683	2.1	2.3	2.6	2.9	3.0
Northern Africa	74,520	86,606	119,719	170,143	247,424	3.0	3.2	3.4	3.7	3.8
Southern Africa	20,318	22,779	29,227	38,399	51,710	2.3	2.4	2.7	2.9	3.0
Tropical South America	129,854	151,523	209,966	295,754	420,972	3.1	3.2	3.4	3.5	3.6
Middle America (Mainland)	56,961	67,485	96,413	140,425	206,814	3.4	3.5	3.7	3.8	3.9
Caribbean	23,068	26,041	33,725	44,540	60,115	2.4	2.5	2.7	2.9	3.1
Melanesia	2,452	2,767	3,612	4,886	6,798	2.4	2.6	2.9	3.2	3.4
Polynesia and Micronesia	1,053	1,229	1,733	2,478	3,544	3.1	3.3	3.6	3.6	3.6

SOURCE: UN Population Division

South Asia, 42 per cent in East Asia (excluding Japan), 17 per cent in Latin America and 7 per cent in Africa.

SOURCE: UN Population Division

INDIVIDUAL RIGHTS
At the individual level, in the more developed as well as the less developed countries, unplanned pregnancies can cause or aggravate conditions of social and economic hardship. High rates of infant mortality, permanent mental impairment resulting from malnutrition in the formative years, social and economic privations—all these bear witness to the problems high fertility can give rise to when household budgets are already at the subsistence level. They are evidence of the strain felt by families when the nurture of each additional child must inevitably be at the expense of those already born.

3A UN Declaration
THE FAMILY

The family is a basic unit of society and the natural environment for the growth and well-being of all its members, particularly children and youth, should be assisted and protected so that it may fully assume its responsibilities within the community. Parents have the exclusive right to determine freely and responsibly the number and spacing of their children.

SOURCE: UN General Assembly 1969 Declaration on Social Progress and Development

3B U Thant
FAMILY RIGHTS

The Universal Declaration of Human Rights describes the family as the natural and fundamental unit of society. It follows that any choice and decision with regard to the size of the family must irrevocably rest with the family itself, and cannot be made by anyone else. But this right of parents to free choice will remain illusory unless they are aware of the alternatives open to them. Hence, the right of every family to information and to the availability of services in this field is increasingly considered as a basic human right and as an indispensable ingredient of human dignity.

SOURCE: 1967 Human Rights Day statement by UN Secretary-General U Thant

3C Teheran Conference
FAMILY RIGHTS

... couples have a basic human right to decide freely and responsibly on the number and spacing of their children and a right to adequate education and information in this respect.

SOURCE: Resolution of the Teheran International Conference on Human Rights (1968)

NATIONAL GOALS
The rate of population growth jeopardises the best efforts of governments for the economic and social development of their peoples.

Food
In the developing countries rapid population growth has stimulated a growing concern over the problem of hunger and malnutrition. Per capita food production in these countries remained practically unchanged between the mid-1950s and mid-1960s in spite of substantial increases in total output. Much hope is placed today in the so-called 'green revolution'. It is possible that, with new agricultural technology, providing a country's minimum food needs will not necessarily have the attributes of a daily crisis; but many qualifications need to be made even to this cautious statement. Agronomists are keenly aware of the need for proper husbandry of the new strains of wheat and rice, of the importance of the right application and combination of inputs, of the need for credit and marketing facilities. Many financial and administrative constraints will

have to be eliminated before yield-increases that have been achieved in certain parts of the developing world can be sustained, and improved upon, over a wider area. Huge social problems will increasingly arise with the transformation of agriculture in the less developed countries. Land-tenure patterns, distribution of agrarian incomes and farm holdings by size, and rates of rural-urban migration are likely to be significantly modified. Rapid population growth seems certain to increase the number of landless, subsistence or disadvantaged sectors of society and to raise the administrative burdens and social costs of absorbing urban arrivals.

In both developed and developing countries the continued intensification and extensification of agriculture to meet the needs of growing populations create major problems of environmental pollution, and soil and water deterioration. Increased use of pesticides and chemical fertilisers may have serious ecological consequences. Large-scale irrigation schemes, the reclamation of marginal land, the clearing of forests, etc, may pose severe threats to the stability of natural ecosystems.

A population growing at

1 per cent doubles itself in	70 years
2 per cent doubles itself in	35 years
2·5 per cent doubles itself in	27 years
3 per cent doubles itself in	23 years
3·5 per cent doubles itself in	20 years

By far the greater part of the additional demand for food over the next 15 years will be due to increases in population, particularly in the developing countries. The population growth factor will require an increase of two-thirds in food supplies over 20 years in the developing countries merely to maintain existing nutrition levels and patterns of consumption. The demand for food in the developing countries as a whole by 1985 will be about 140 per cent greater than the 1962 level. At least two-thirds of this increase will come from population growth. Another third will result from assumed higher per capita consumption as income levels rise. To meet projected demand, the present trend of between 2·6 per cent annual increase in food produced in developing countries and retained for domestic consumption would need to be stepped up to 4·3 per cent per year.

Fig 4 Trends in food production and population in the developing regions

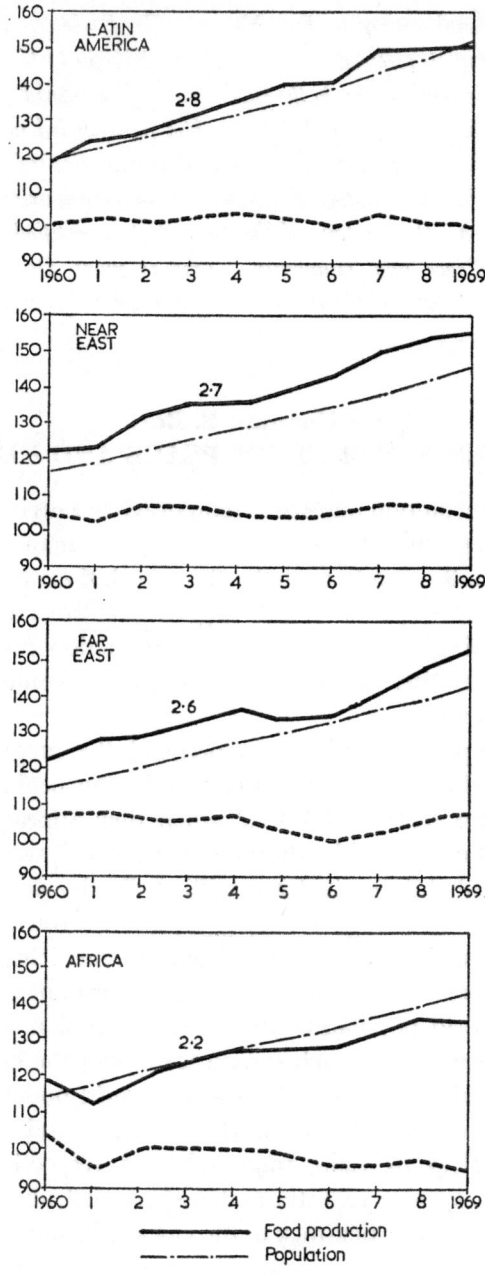

SOURCE: FAO, *State of Food and Agriculture* (1970)

On 10 December 1970 Dr Norman E. Borlaug, distinguished American scientist, received the Nobel Peace Prize in Oslo, Norway, for his remarkable contribution to the enlargement of the world's food supply, particularly in underdeveloped nations. His research led to the development and widespread use of high-yielding varieties of wheat, now produced in Mexico, India, Pakistan and other countries. In accepting the award, Dr Borlaug delivered a lecture entitled 'The Green Revolution, Peace and Humanity'. This is what Dr Borlaug had to say in that lecture about the relation between food and population.

4 Dr Norman E. Borlaug
THE GREEN REVOLUTION, PEACE AND HUMANITY

The green revolution has won a temporary success in man's war against hunger and deprivation; it has given man a breathing space. If fully implemented, the revolution can provide sufficient food for sustenance during the next three decades. But the frightening power of human reproduction must also be curbed; otherwise, the success of the green revolution will be ephemeral only.

Most people still fail to comprehend the magnitude and menace of the 'Population Monster'. In the beginning there were but two, Adam and Eve; when they appeared on this earth is still questionable. By the time of Christ, world population had probably reached 250 million. But between then and now population has grown to 3·5 billion. Growth has been especially fast since the advent of modern medicine. If it continues to increase at the estimated present rate of 2 per cent a year, the world population will reach 6·5 billion by the year 2000. Currently, with each second, or tick of the clock, about 2·2 additional people are added to the world population. The rhythm of increase will accelerate to 2·7, 3·03 and 4·0 for each tick of the clock by 1980, 1990 and 2000, respectively, unless man becomes more realistic and preoccupied about this impending doom. The tick-tock of the clock will continually grow louder and more menacing each decade. Where will it all end?

SOURCE: Nobel Peace Prize lecture by Dr Norman Borlaug

Dr Borlaug has also given the following warning.

The time is a quarter to midnight. . . . If we hesitate or falter, the monster—rapid population growth—will destroy the world.

Education
The number of children enrolled in the primary schools of the less developed countries rose 150 per cent during the 15 years from 1950 to 1965, and the percentage of all children 6–12 years old who were in school rose from less than 40 per cent to more than 60 per cent. This marked increase in enrolment ratios reflected in large measure the value placed on education by people of all classes and income groups in the developing countries.

It is estimated that the child population in the developing regions during the 1970s will continue to constitute 40–45 per cent of the total population, and sometimes more. The number of children of school age (5–14) will increase from 560 millions in 1965 to over 1,000 million by the end of the century, even if fertility is substantially reduced. This means that almost intolerable burdens will be placed upon the educational system, even to maintain the present unsatisfactory school attendance. It means that even with a major allocation of resources to education, ie construction of schools, training of teachers, etc, the absolute number of illiterates—already more than one-third of all the adults in the world—is likely to increase rather than diminish. In fact, between 1960 and 1970, the absolute total of illiterates increased by 70 millions because of the rise in population.

Health
Albert Einstein has said: 'Progress of hygiene and medicine has completely altered the earlier precarious equilibrium of the quantitative stability of the human race. I am therefore firmly convinced that a powerful attempt to solve this tremendous problem is of urgent necessity'.

Fig 5 School enrolment

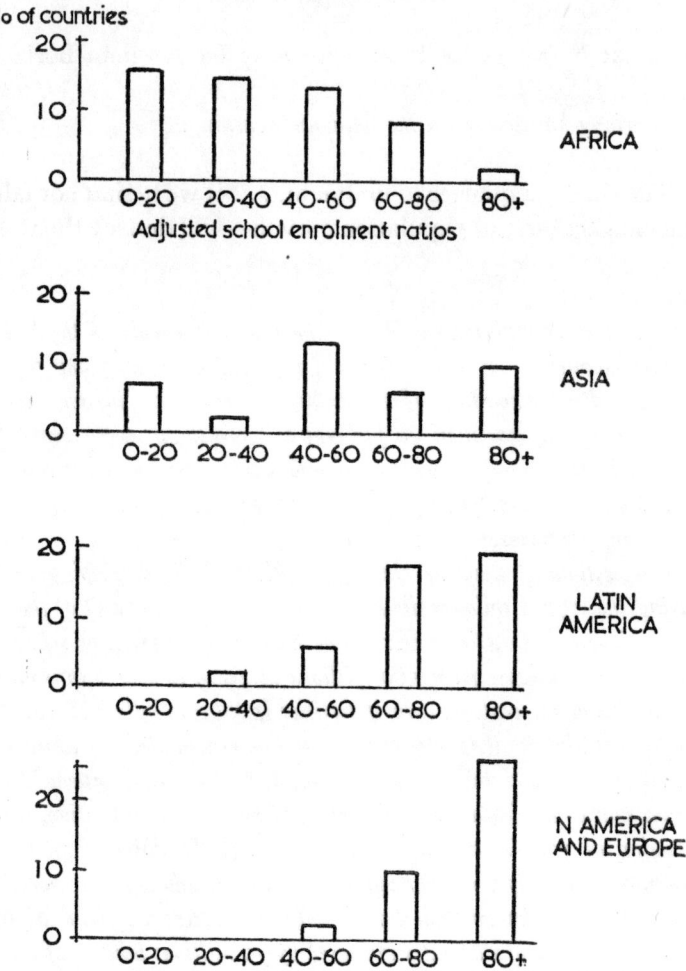

SOURCE: National Academy of Sciences (US), *Rapid Population Growth*

Public health technology applied on a mass scale in the developing countries has indeed reduced death rates dramatically. Yet the level of personal health services for the individual and the community varies widely and, in general, remains far below the levels of the more developed regions. High fertility forces health ministries to run fast in order to stay in the same place—let alone improve services. For the next 20 years at least, the demand for health services will outrun the supply by any measure such as doctor/population ratios or number of hospital beds. Rapidly growing population combined with growing aspirations makes this inevitable. The age and geographical distribution of the population also affect the health services. In a high-fertility community the primary stress on health services will be the care of mothers and children. The problems of medical treatment for infants are substantially greater than the problems of treating young adults, and hence care of the young requires a higher doctor/population ratio than the care of people aged 15–45. The levels of personal health services are usually much higher in urban than in rural areas, both in terms of numbers and quality.

Rapid population growth and its accompanying rapid urbanisation are injurious to health, though it may be difficult to isolate the effects of crowding from other conditions such as poverty, poor nutrition, poor housing and pollution. These problems, of course, are in themselves partly a consequence of rapid population growth.

Urbanisation

It is estimated that the world's urban population, which was 33 per cent of the total world population in 1960, will be 46 per cent in 1980 and 51 per cent in 2000. At the beginning of the twenty-first century the urban population of Latin America may include 80 per cent of the region's total population, making that region more urbanised than Europe, while the urban population of North America will reach 87 per cent of the total. The percentage of urban population during the 1960–2000 period will grow from 23 to 40 in East Africa, from 18 to 35 in South Asia and from 18 to 30 in Africa as a whole. In the year 2000 it is projected that 62 per cent of the world's urban population will be living in the regions now described as developing. The corresponding figure for 1960 was only 41 per cent. In 1900 probably no more than a quarter of the world's population lived in urban settlements.

High rates of population growth and rapid urbanisation are inevitably linked. Today, when the population growth rates of urban centres often exceed an annual average increase of 6 per cent and sometimes reach

10 per cent or more, many developing countries are now in the most critical period, and others are on the threshold of transformation from primarily rural to primarily urban societies.

Fig 6 Time relationships between a birth and future service requirements

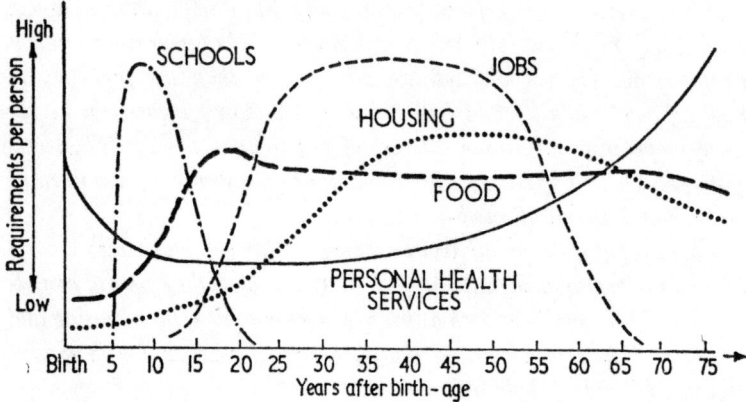

SOURCE: National Academy of Sciences (US), *Rapid Population Growth*

It is characteristic of the urbanisation process that the more it progresses the more significant is the part represented by large cities among the total urban population. The overconcentration of population in certain centres and subsequent overcrowding in squatter settlements and slums in developing as well as developed countries creates social problems and environmental deterioration. Air, water and land pollution, and damage to the ecological balance of the environment have become major problems of urban settlements in developed countries, and are beginning to affect developing countries as well.

Housing

At the beginning of the 1960s the United Nations, in its proposals for the first development decade, estimated that around ten dwelling units per 1,000 inhabitants had to be built each year in the developing countries in order to offset obsolescence and to cope with the urban population growth throughout the decade. In most developing countries less than two houses per 1,000 inhabitants are being built each year.

Fig 7 Growth of world population and urban population in various categories, 1920–80

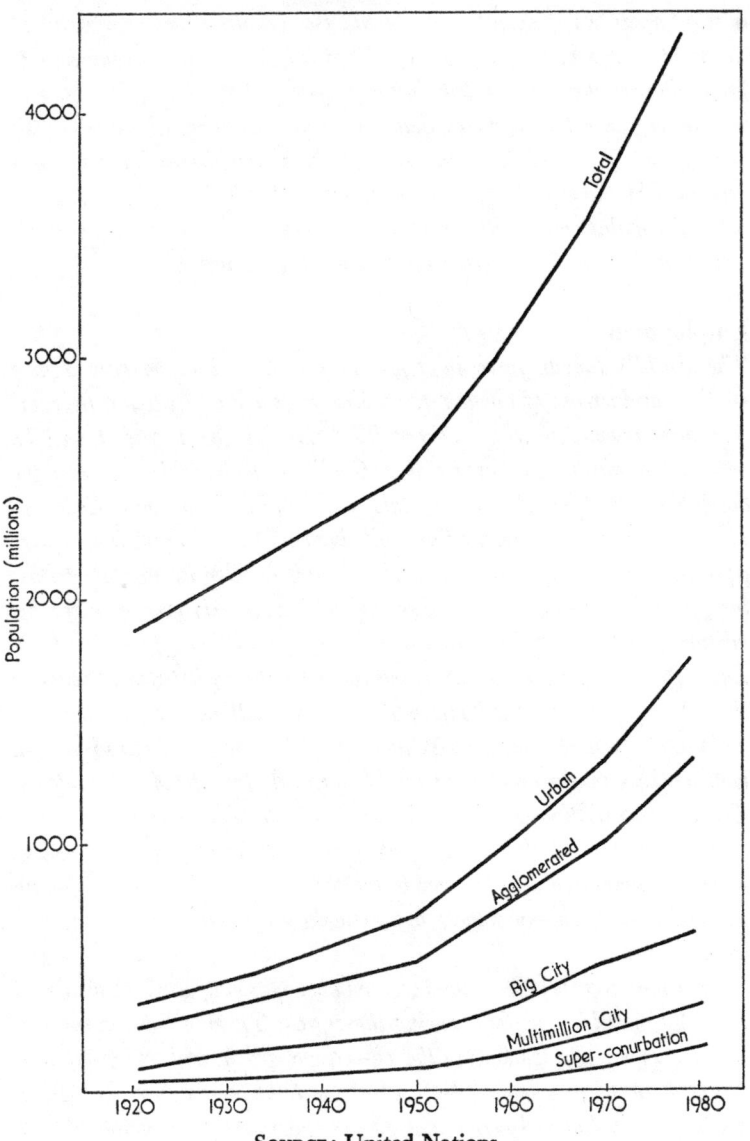

SOURCE: United Nations

In Latin America the housing deficit is about 20 million units; in Asia and the Far East it is about 22 million in urban areas and 125 million in rural areas (as of 1960). In industrialised countries the average rate of construction has been below the suggested targets. Today a considerable proportion of the world's population is poorly housed and is likely to remain so, since the resources that are at present being allocated to the housing sector are modest compared to the rising demand for housing generated by the rapidly growing population. With the world's projected rate of population growth, 1,100–1,400 million new dwelling units would need to be built before the end of this century.

Employment

The world's labour force in 1970 was estimated to be over 1,500 million, an increase of about 200 million since 1960. By 1980 the total may have reached nearly 1,800 million. During the 1970s it will be necessary to absorb an increase of 226 million in the labour force of the developing countries, the bulk of this total coming from South East and East Asia, where the labour force will increase from 804 million to over 970 million, roughly 20 per cent. Although smaller in absolute terms, the forseeable increase in the other regions is relatively even greater: 32 million (23 per cent) in Africa and nearly 30 million (32 per cent) in Latin America. In the industrialised countries the anticipated increase in the labour force during the 1970s is about 56 million (11 per cent).

Within the next three decades there could be more than 1,000 million new workers in the developing world, with all the attendant problems. Already 300 million new jobs will need to be provided during the UN's second development decade, to make good the backlog of 76 million already unemployed and to provide for the expected 226 million growth in the labour force—and these figures make no provision for 'disguised' unemployment.

Of equal significance is the large number of young workers who will swell the world labour force during the 1970s. There will be an increase of some 21 million workers in the 15–19 age group, and this group will represent in 1980 some 15 per cent of the total labour force in Africa, 15 per cent in Latin America and 12 per cent in Asia, as compared with 9 per cent in Europe and 8 per cent in North America. The problem of finding useful and productive employment for young people in the developing countries will be one of the most urgent and challenging for governments in the years to come.

TABLE 8

Level of unemployment and underemployment in developing countries, excluding mainland China

(in millions and percent)

	1970	1980	1970		1980	
Fully employed	504	592	75·3%		70·5%	
Underemployed	130	200	19·4 ↘		23·8 ↘	
Employed	634	792	94·7%	24·7%	94·3%	29·5%
Unemployed	36	48	5·3 ↗		5·7 ↗	
Total Labour Force	670	840	100·0%		100·0%	

SOURCE: World Bank and ILO

Environment

The environmental impact of population growth differs between regions and between countries within regions. In the developing countries the ills caused by poverty leave little room for concern about, or expenditures on, the environment in ways that now preoccupy many people in rich countries. The environmental problems of the less developed countries arise much more from rapid population growth combined with a lack of technology than from rising incomes and the presence of new technology. Rapidly rising populations bring unwelcome pressure to bear on resources, eg extension of cropping into rain-fed areas that are at best suitable only for grazing, random deforestation, etc. The very rapid spread of new technology, eg the 'green revolution' designed to feed rising population, may have secondary effects on the environment to a degree and extent yet unknown.

The effect of rapid population growth on the economic position and prospects clearly has environmental consequences as well. The contamination of water supplies by sewage, rampant and unplanned urbanisation, health and disease problems in both city and countryside—all these reflect the very lack of development that is at the root of so many poor countries' problems

In the more industrialised countries, and in those countries where the process of industrialisation is already under way, environmental problems manifest themselves rather differently. It is not easy to distinguish the extent to which industrial pollution, problems of solid waste, marine pollution, etc, are a function of population increase. Certainly rising standards of living and growing affluence, combined with the force of technology, exert a 'multiplier effect', such that even relatively modest increases in the populations of so-called developed countries may have a

Fig 8   Comparison between developed and less developed world in population and GNP

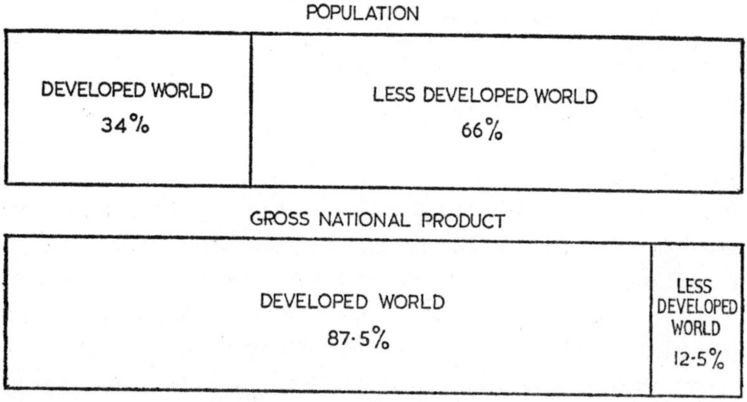

POPULATION

DEVELOPED WORLD 34%	LESS DEVELOPED WORLD 66%

GROSS NATIONAL PRODUCT

DEVELOPED WORLD 87·5%	LESS DEVELOPED WORLD 12·5%

SOURCE: United Nations Association of the United States of America: *World Population—a report of a National Policy Panel*

quite disproportionate effect on the 'eco-system' as a whole. Environmentally the growing populations of Europe, North America, Japan and the Soviet Union constitute the truly global threat, not the populations of Africa, Asia and Latin America; for it is in the so-called 'advanced' industrial nations that growing populations make the most impact upon terrestrial eco-systems and upon the scarce resources of the biosphere (see Fig 8). These nations are the rich nations, whose technological achievements are the highest, and it is their patterns of production and consumption which, when allied with steadily increasing populations, have led to the present acute environmental problems.

Increase in GDP

Between 1960 and 1968, the developing countries increased their gross domestic product (GDP) by an annual average rate of 4·7 per cent. However, their population increased by 2·6 per cent, which meant that this accelerating rate of population growth held down the rate of growth of GDP per head of population to an average of 2·1 per cent.

Fig 9 GNP growth rate for the four regions of (1) Africa, (2) East Asia* (3) Latin America, and (4) the Near East and South Asia

	TOTAL GNP (% change)	GNP per capita (% change)
AFRICA	5·2	2·7
EAST ASIA	12·4	10·1
LATIN AMERICA	6·2	3·2
NEAR EAST AND S ASIA	6·0	3·5

SOURCE: USAID

* Average of per cent changes in 1969 and 1968. Non-Communist countries.
Note: East Asia includes Japan. Africa includes South Africa.

Growth in income is dealt with in the introduction to the World Bank's paper 'Population Planning'. For further discussion of the World Bank's role in the field of population, see p 201.

5 World Bank
POPULATION PLANNING

The purpose of economic development is to make possible higher living standards for individual men, women and children. A rising standard of living means a growing ability to afford both the material and non-material benefits which a modernized economy makes possible. For most people in most countries, however, the first requirements are more and better food, improved access to education and health care, and more opportunity for gainful employment.

Despite its limitations, one of the best avilable measures of economic progress toward these goals is the growth of per capita income. This is the growth of national income, adjusted for growth of population. Thus the relationship between the growth of a nation's income and that of its population is fundamental to the improvement of human welfare.

While neither the causes nor the effects in this relationship are fully understood, one central fact is clear: the higher the rate of population growth, the more difficult it is to raise per capita income. Today the world's population is growing much faster than at any time in history. This simple fact led the Pearson Commission to say, in 1969, that 'No other phenomenon casts a darker shadow over the prospects for international development than the staggering growth of population.'

The problems created by the large numbers and high growth rates of population concern both the world as a whole and individual countries. Both more and less developed countries confront such universal questions as the ultimate size of population the world can sustain and the rate at which the limit will be approached. The earth can undoubtedly support substantially more than the 3·6 billion people now living on it. But there is great doubt about its ability to sustain unlimited numbers at decent standards of living, which a majority do not have even now.

The World Bank's concern, however, is not with ultimate numbers but with the developmental impact of population growth. Development does not mean more people, but higher living standards and greater welfare for however many there may be. The Bank entered the field chiefly because it became convinced that the attempt to raise living standards in a great many developing countries was being seriously undermined if not thwarted. The Bank has no fixed ideas as to how large the population of individual countries ought to be. But it is convinced that in the great majority of developing countries, the faster the rate of population growth, the slower will be the improvement of living standards. Within the last few years, the governments of more than 26 countries have indicated that they share this belief by adopting official policies to slow their population growth.

There is another important reason for the Bank's entry into the population field. It concerns human welfare, and particularly health. There is strong evidence that where children have been well spaced, both they and their mothers enjoy better health and experience lower mortality rates. It does not follow, of course, that parents will necessarily choose to space their children or to have fewer of them, if given the chance to do so.

Many governments feel, however, that people should be given the choice if it is possible to bring it to them, and the Bank is prepared to help them do so. Experience suggests that if couples are given this voluntary choice their own family-size decisions will tend to slow the rate of population growth. Yet no one can predict whether the general response will develop strongly or quickly enough to give governments substantial help in attaining their development objectives.

SOURCE: World Bank, 'Population Planning'

INTERNATIONAL IMPLICATIONS

In 1968, the United Nations Association of the United States of America established a National Policy Panel to consider the question of World Population under the chairmanship of John D. Rockefeller 3rd. The panel reported in May 1969, recommending major new initiatives to be taken by the United Nations and its system of agencies in this field. This is what the panel had to say about the international implications of the population problem.

6A United Nations Association of the United States
THE POPULATION CRISIS IS THE WORLD'S CONCERN

The population crisis is the world's concern. It is as important as peace itself. To what extent territorial aggression is a function of population pressures, or military adventurism a smokescreen to hide the real failures of development, cannot be said with certainty. What can be said is that this is an age when the internal stability of countries is constantly threatened by the massive disaffection or disappointment of those whose expectations have not been met; it is an age when the growing polarisation between rich and poor nations makes the conduct of orderly external relations increasingly difficult. If it is true that internal stability and external order are influenced, however indirectly, by the rate of population growth, then the commitment of the international community to the cause of peace should be matched by a parallel commitment to population planning.

There are other good reasons for international interest in the population problem. No nation can live in isolation. The world is only just beginning to realise the dangers involved in the changing and complex relationship between man and his environment. Contamination of the streams and oceans, erosion of the soil, destruction of vegetation, the devouring of open space, the rise in the concentration of carbon dioxide in the atmosphere, indiscriminate use of poisonous pesticides and synthetic detergents, the disposal of radio-active waste—these are problems which have vast international implications. To deal with effects without dealing also with causes is inadequate and superficial. One of the causes, perhaps the root cause, of the threat to our environment is the demands made by expanding populations in developed and developing world alike (see Fig 10). The fact that, at the present time, we have only the haziest ideas of the nature of the interrelationships involved should not provide an excuse for inaction. If the present world population of $3\frac{1}{2}$ billion is allowed to grow to 7 billion or more, our understanding of these things and of possible ways of mitigating their impact may come too late to be of much comfort.

FACTS AND FIGURES AND THEIR MEANING

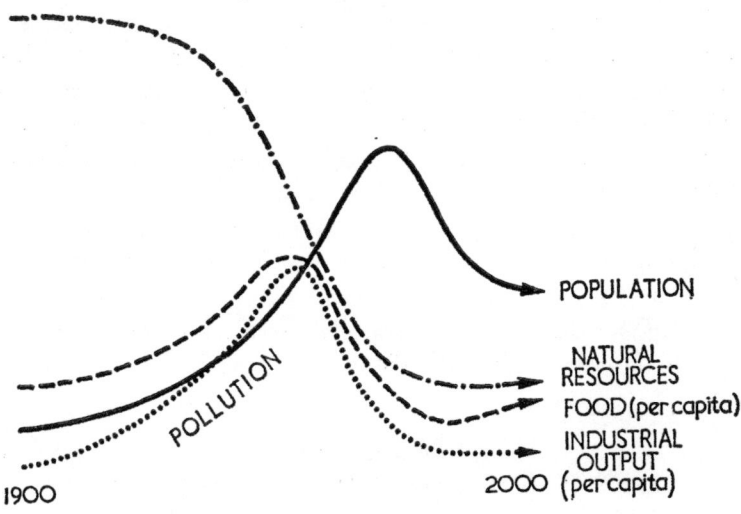

Fig 10   Projection for disaster

SOURCE: Adapted from computer-output chart in 'The Limits to Growth' report (see p 67)

TABLE 9
Current and ultimate stationary populations on assumption that birth rates drop immediately to stationary level

	Current	Ultimate	Percent increase to ultimate
Canada 1968	20,264,000	28,562,000	40·9
Chile 1965	8,584,000	12,916,000	50·5
Colombia 1965	17,993,000	29,786,000	65·5
Ecuador 1965	5,109,000	8,518,000	66·7
Ireland 1968	2,910,000	3,684,000	26·6
Italy 1966	53,128,000	62,189,000	17·1
Trinidad and Tobago 1967	1,015,000	1,633,000	60·9
United States 1966	195,857,000	259,490,000	32·5

SOURCE: National Academy of Sciences (US), *Rapid Population Growth*

In June 1972, the United Nations Conference on the Human Environment met in Stockholm. The Conference adopted a Declaration on the Human Environment. It 'proclaimed', inter alia, that 'the natural growth of population continuously presents problems for the preservation of the environment, and adequate policies and measures should be adopted, as appropriate, to face these problems'. It went on to state the 'common conviction' that 'demographic policies, which are without prejudice to basic human rights and which are deemed appropriate by Governments concerned, should be applied in those regions where the rate of population growth or excessive population concentrations are likely to have adverse effects on the environment or development, or where low population density may prevent improvement of the human environment and impede development'.

One of the best speeches in the general debate was made by Mrs Indira Gandhi, the prime minister of India.

6B Indira Gandhi
LIFE IS ONE AND THE WORLD IS ONE

One cannot be truly human and civilized unless one looks upon not only fellow-man but all creation with the eyes of a friend. . . .

It is sad that in country after country, progress should become synonymous with an assault on nature. We who are a part of nature and dependent on her for every need, speak constantly about 'exploiting' nature. . . . I remember Edward Thompson, a British writer and a good friend of India, once telling Mr. Gandhi that wild life was fast disappearing. Remarked the Mahatma—'It is decreasing in the jungles but it is increasing in the towns!'. . .

As we struggle to create a better life for our people, we cannot indulge in . . . practices (of exploiting the labor of the masses) even for a worthwhile purpose. We are bound by our own ideals. We owe allegiance to the principles of the rights of workers and the norms enshrined in the charters of international organizations. Above all, we are answerable to the millions of politically awakened citizens in our countries. All these make progress costlier and more complicated.

On the one hand the rich look askance at our continuing poverty—on the other they warn us against their own methods.

We do not wish to impoverish the environment any further and yet we cannot for a moment forget the grim poverty of large numbers of people. Are not poverty and need the greatest polluters? For instance, unless we are in a position to provide employment and purchasing power for the daily necessities of the tribal people and those who live in or around our jungles, we cannot prevent them from combing the forest for food and livelihood; from poaching and from despoiling the vegetation. When they themselves feel deprived, how can we urge the preservation of animals? How can we speak to those who live in villages and in slums about keeping the oceans, the rivers and the air clean when their own lives are contaminated at the source? The environment cannot be improved in conditions of poverty. Nor can poverty be eradicated without the use of science and technology.

Must there be conflict between technology and a truly better world or between enlightenment of the spirit and a higher standard of living? . . .

I am reminded of an incident in one of our tribal areas. The vociferous demand of elder tribal chiefs that their customs should be left undisturbed found support from noted anthropologists. In its anxiety that the majority should not submerge the many ethnical, racial and cultural groups in our country, the Government of India largely accepted this advice. I was amongst those who entirely approved. However, a visit to a remote part of our northeast frontier brought me in touch with a different point of view—the protest of the younger elements that while the rest of India was on the way to modernization they were being preserved as museum pieces. Could we not say the same to the affluent nations? . . .

We should re-order our priorities and move away from the . . . model which seems to have given a higher place to things rather than to persons and which has increased our wants rather than our enjoyment. We should have a more comprehensive approach to life, centred on man not as a statistic but an individual with many sides to his personality. The solution of these problems cannot be isolated phenomena of marginal importance but must be an integral part of the unfolding of the very process of development.

The extreme forms in which questions of population or environmental pollution are posed, obscure the total view of political, economic and social situations. The Government of India ... believe(s) that planned families will make for a healthier and more conscious population. But we know also that no program of population control can be effective without education and without a visible rise in the standard of living. ...

It is an oversimplification to blame all the world's problems on increasing population. Countries with but a small fraction of the world population consume the bulk of the world's production of minerals, fossil fuels, and so on. ...

The inherent conflict is not between conservation and development but between environment and the reckless exploitation of man and earth in the name of efficiency. ...

Cause of the crisis

All the 'isms' of the modern age—even those which in theory disown the private profit principle—assume that man's cardinal interest is acquisition. The profit motive, individual or collective, seems to overshadow all else. This overriding concern with Self and Today is the basic cause of the ecological crisis.

It is clear that the environmental crisis which is confronting the world, will profoundly alter the future destiny of our planet. No one among us, whatever our status, strength or circumstance, can remain unaffected. The process of change challenges present international policies. Will the growing awareness of 'one earth' and 'one environment' guide us to the concept of 'one humanity'? Will there be a more equitable sharing of environmental costs and greater international interest in the accelerated progress of the less developed world? Or will it remain confined to a narrow concern, based on exclusive self-sufficiency?

Life is one

Life is one and the world is one, and all these questions are interlinked. The population explosion, poverty, ignorance and disease, the pollution of our surroundings, the stockpiling of nuclear weapons and biological and chemical agents of destruction are all parts of a vicious circle. Each is important and urgent but dealing with them one by one would be wasted effort. . . .

SOURCE: Mrs Gandhi's speech to UN Conference on Human Environment (June 1972)

In the spring of 1972, before the UN Conference on the Human Environment in Stockholm, two reports were published which had a profound impact. The first appeared in Britain in the January 1972 issue of The Ecologist. *It was called 'A Blueprint for Survival'. In March 1972, the report by the Club of Rome known as 'The Limits to Growth' was made public. Both reports argued the need for a stable society: stable in respect of output and stable in respect of population. Here are some excerpts from the latter.*

7 'The Limits to Growth Report'
ON REACHING A STATE OF GLOBAL EQUILIBRIUM

If the present growth trends in world population, industrialization, pollution, food production and resource depletion continue unchanged, the limits to growth on this planet will be reached sometime within the next one hundred years. The most probable result will be a rather sudden and uncontrollable decline in both population and industrial capacity.

It is possible to alter these growth trends and to establish a condition of ecological and economic stability that is sustainable far into the future. The state of global equilibrium could be designed so that the basic material needs of each person on earth are satisfied and each person has an equal opportunity to realize his individual human potential.

If the world's people decide to strive for this second outcome rather than the first, the sooner they begin working to attain it, the greater will be their chances of success.

There may be much disagreement with the statement that population and capital growth must stop *soon*. But virtually no one will argue that material growth on this planet can go on forever. At this point in man's history, the choice posed above is still available in almost every sphere of human activity. Man can still choose his limits and stop when he pleases by weakening some of the strong pressures that cause capital and population growth, or by instituting counterpressures, or both. Such counterpressures will probably not be entirely pleasant. They will certainly involve profound changes in the social and economic structures that have been deeply impressed into human culture by centuries of growth. The alternative is to wait until the price of technology becomes more than society can pay, or until the side-effects of technology suppress growth themselves, or until problems arise that have no technical solutions. At any of those points the choice of limits will be gone. Growth will be stopped by pressures that are not of human choosing, and that may be very much worse than those which society might choose for itself.

Technology can relieve the symptoms of a problem without affecting the underlying causes. Faith in technology as the ultimate solution to all problems can thus divert our attention from the most fundamental problem—the problem of growth in a finite system—and prevent us from taking effective action to solve it.

On the other hand, our intent is certainly not to brand technology as evil or futile or unnecessary. We are technologists ourselves, working in a technological institution. We strongly believe that many of the technological developments mentioned here—recycling, pollution control devices, contraceptives—will be absolutely vital to the future of human society *if they are combined with deliberate checks on growth.* We would deplore an unreasoned rejection of the benefits of technology as strongly as we argue here against an unreasoned acceptance of them.

We have, after much discussion, decided to call the state of constant population and capital by the term 'equilibrium'. Equilibrium means a state of balance or equality between opposing forces. The opposing forces are those causing population and capital stock to increase (high desired family size, low birth-control effectiveness, high rate of capital investment) and those causing population and capital stock to decrease (lack of food, pollution, high rate of depreciation or obsolescence). The word 'capital' should be understood to mean service, industrial and agricultural capital combined. *Thus the most basic definition of the state of global equilibrium is that population and capital are essentially stable, with the forces tending to increase or decrease them in a carefully controlled balance.*

At the limit, of course, no population or capital level can be maintained forever, but that limit is very far away in time if resources are managed wisely and if there is a sufficiently long time horizon in planning. Let us take as a reasonable time horizon the expected lifetime of a child born into the world tomorrow—70 years if proper food and medical care are supplied. Since most people spend a large part of their time and energy raising children, they might choose as a minimum goal that the society left to those children can be maintained for the full span of the children's lives.

If society's time horizon is as long as 70 years, the permissible population and capital levels may not be too different from those existing today. The rates would be considerably different from those of today, however. Any society would undoubtedly prefer that the death rate be low rather than high, since a long, healthy life seems to be a universal human desire. To maintain equilibrium with long life expectancy, the birth rate then must also be low. It would be best, too, if the capital investment and depreciation rates were low, because the lower they are, the less resource depletion and pollution there will be.

By choosing a fairly long time horizon for its existence, and a long average lifetime as a desirable goal, we have now arrived at a minimum set of requirements for the state of global equilibrium. They are:

(1.) *The capital plant and the population are constant in size.* The birth rate equals the death rate and the capital investment rate equals the depreciation rate.

(2.) *All input and output rates—births, deaths, investment, and depreciation—are kept to a minimum.*

(3.) *The levels of capital and population and the ratio of the two are set in accordance with the values of the society.* They may be deliberately revised and slowly adjusted as the advance of technology creates new options.

What would life be like in such an equilibrium state? Would innovation be stifled? Would society be locked into the patterns of inequality and injustice we see in the world today? Discussion of these questions must proceed on the basis of mental models, for there is no formal model of social conditions in the equilibrium state. No one can predict what sort of institutions mankind might develop under these new conditions. There is, of course, no guarantee that the new society would be much better or even much different from that which exists today. It seems possible, however, that a society released from struggling with the many problems caused by growth may have more energy and ingenuity available for solving other problems. In fact, we believe that the evolution of a society that favors innovation and technological development, a society based on equality and justice, is far more likely to evolve in a state of global equilibrium than it is in the state of growth we are experiencing today.

The concept of a society in a steady state of economic and ecological equilibrium may appear easy to grasp, although the reality is so distant from our experience as to require a Copernican revolution of the mind. Translating the idea into deed, though, is a task filled with overwhelming difficulties and complexities. We can talk seriously about where to start only when the message of 'The Limits to Growth', and its sense of extreme urgency, are accepted by a large body of scientific, political, and popular opinion in many countries. The transition in any case is likely to be painful, and it will make extreme demands on human ingenuity and determination. As we have mentioned, only the conviction that there is no other avenue to survival can liberate the moral, intellectual, and creative forces required to initiate this unprecedented human undertaking.

SOURCE: *New York Times* (13 March 1972)

PART TWO

The Developing World

In its publication A Concise Summary of the World Population Situation in 1970 *the United Nations writes:*

The degree of government involvement has not necessarily been a measure of the effectiveness of family-planning programmes actually implemented. More often than not, direct official involvement, through the enactment of laws or the establishment of official agencies, has been the outcome of activities and programmes already in existence for some time at less official levels and which have found support in public opinion. The exact official position is sometimes difficult to determine. Nevertheless, by the end of 1969, the Governments of about thirty less developed countries, comprising almost two-thirds of the combined population of the less developed regions, had adopted national family-planning programmes as integral parts of their development policies.

The situation has been summarised in Table 10 by the Population Council, in Population and Family Planning Programmes: A fact book, *by Dorothy Nortman (1971). The difference in totals (the UN says 'almost two-thirds', while the Population Council's figure is nearer three-quarters, for the proportion of developing countries' population covered by official anti-natalist policies) reflects in part the difficulties of categorisation, in part the difference in the dates of the surveys.*

TABLE 10

Number of countries and distribution of the population in the major regions of the developing world, by governmental position on family planning programs and policies

Governmental position	All developing countries*	Africa	Latin America†	East Asia‡	Balance of Asia‖
	NUMBER OF COUNTRIES				
All positions	102	42	23	5	32
Official antinatalist policy and a family planning program	24	7	5	3	10
Support of family planning activities but no official policy	23	7	13	1	1
Little or no support of family planning activities and no official antinatalist policy	55	28	5	1	21
	POPULATION (IN MILLIONS)				
All positions	2,542	344	256	820	1,122
Official antinatalist policy and a family planning program	1,838	141	11	786	966
Support of family planning activities but no official policy	213	47	84	4	12
Little or no support of family planning activities and no official antinatalist policy	491	156	161	30	144
	PER CENT DISTRIBUTION OF POPULATION				
All positions	100	100	100	100	100
Official antinatalist policy and a family planning program	72	41	4	96	86
Support of family planning activities but no official policy	9	14	33	0.1	1
Little or no support of family planning activities and no official antinatalist policy	19	45	63	4	13

* Classification primarily on the basis of level of fertility.

† Comprises the Caribbean area and Central and South America, except for Argentina and Uruguay, both of which have low fertility.

‡ Comprises China (Mainland), Hong Kong, North Korea, South Korea, and Taiwan; excludes Japan, which has low fertility. Population for China (Mainland) based on the United Nations estimate of 740 million. A more likely estimate exceeds 850 million.

‖ Excludes Israel, which has low fertility.

SOURCE: *Population Council, 1971*

Table 11 divides the population of the developing countries, apart from mainland China, into categories according to fertility and mortality levels.

TABLE 11
Population distribution in millions in developing countries (excluding mainland China) by fertility and mortality levels, 1970

Deaths per 1,000 population	Births per 1,000 population	Africa No	%	Asia No	%	Latin America No	%
High (over 25)	High (over 25)	27·1	8·0	17·0	1·4	—	—
Falling (15–25)	High (over 40)	306·9	90·1	978·5	82·6	23·9	8·4
Low (less than 15)	High (over 40)	5·0	1·5	76·3	6·5	112·4	39·9
Low (less than 15)	Falling	1·4	0·4	112·2	9·5	145·4	51·7
	Total	340·4	100·0	1184·0	100·0	281·7	100·0

Note: Due to incomplete birth and death data, 5 African countries with a population total of 42·4 million, and 4 Asian countries with a population total of 26·1 million had to be excluded.

SOURCES of basic data: United Nations, *Population and Vital Statistics Report*, January 1971; *Monthly Bulletin of Statistics*, August 1971; and Population Reference Bureau, *1970 World Population Data Sheet*—supplied by World Bank

ASIA

From the standpoint of population growth as a world problem, developments in Asia are of the first importance. In fact the Governments of China (mainland), India, Pakistan and the Republic of Korea were the first on record as early as the 1950s, with policies aimed to facilitate fertility reductions.

In all the Asian countries with a population exceeding 100 million, family planning is now being promoted by Government agencies. In some other countries Governments subsidise family-planning programmes or projects undertaken by semi-official or unofficial agencies, and in still others Governments permit, or view with favour, projects carried out by unofficial bodies without active official participation.

China
Here are two long pieces which give some indication of what it means to translate an official policy into actual practice. The first is by Han

Suyin, MD, *a doctor and an author who knows China well. Though demographic and census data from China are notoriously difficult to obtain, there seems to be no doubt about the effectiveness of the Chinese approach to family planning.*

8 Han Suyin
FAMILY PLANNING IN CHINA

We may date the beginning of planned parenthood campaigns to 1956. In that year the launching of family planning drives in Peking was done by posters, public meetings, films, and the wide availability of contraceptives with contraceptive advice. This was very quickly followed by similar movements in many large cities; and it had a double effect; it broke the taboos on discussion of such matters; the films shown helped to educate a great many people.

Family planning took well among the leaders, the intellectuals, the more educated sections; but in 1956 China still had a great amount of illiteracy to combat in the countryside; workers in the factories were being educated too, but not all of them were of the same standard. And finally, this preliminary campaign with its emphasis on medical and social aspects lacked the political content which Chairman Mao, in his great and wise leadership, would always put to the fore in all matters; for without 'politics to the fore' no movement, no solution of any problems could go ahead on the clear, definite line which would relate it closely to the aspects of service to the people.

When the family planning teams went to the countryside, at first the reception was quite different from that in the cities. Instead of prompt acceptance, hesitancy, even fear, had been experienced. And this is quite understandable. After all, the poor peasants, the majority population, had been subject to tremendous oppression, misery and exploitation in the recent past; for many decades, they had had to sell their children in times of famine, hoping that those who bought them would look after them. There had been female infanticide in the countryside due to the extreme hardship. In many families, nearly all the babies born died; the infant mortality rate was extremely high.

Women's groups active
The Women's Federation, which I visited in 1959 and again in 1960, carried on family planning education, producing leaflets and printed matter on the subject as well as direct education through women's organizations everywhere; but actually much of the effort in that respect did not reach further than the county town or small township, or the communes in the immediate vicinity of a city. Cadres, intellectuals who went to the countryside after 1958, following Chairman Mao's great call to the intellectuals to go to the countryside, also brought planned parenthood education with them. By and large, however, the rural population did not actually practise family planning. In the factories, however, and among the workers education in planned parenthood began to take root and to spread after 1958.

In the cities, family planning was now firmly implanted; and here the street committees also played an active part in promoting it. Abortions which are legal in China were performed more extensively. I visited several maternity hospitals where abortions were performed, at the demand of both husband and wife. *Already a young generation was manifesting itself in which medical ideas of health and planned parenthood went hand in hand.*

It was through the socialist education movement, which started in 1963 at the inspiration of Chairman Mao Tse-tung, that planned parenthood saw a fresh start; it went hand in hand with the setting up of mobile medical teams (in 1965) and with socialist education. From then on it became part of the construction and building of the new man and the new socialist society, and this set the whole idea of planned parenthood upon a solid basis in the communes.

Malthusianism rejected

In China, it was imperative that there should not be any such economic coercion or pressure; the rejection of the Malthusian theories of 'overpopulation' being the cause of poverty was essential. It was necessary that planned parenthood should be based upon the emancipation of the woman, her equality, her right to study and participation in all political decisions, and her heightened social consciousness. Planned parenthood and marriage are factors for the promotion of a socialist society, but they must be based on full equality of both partners, self-respect, and knowledge. It is therefore essential that the masses themselves should grasp all the factors of health work, and themselves carry out the programs.

The political and economic emancipation of women, therefore, was a requisite for any successful mass campaign of family planning—not only change in the structure of society, but change in thinking, in moral values, in deep-rooted customs of millions of people. This necessarily takes time and unremitting effort.

In 1962 and after, many factories in China were popularizing family planning in many ways—through male sterilization as well as through other techniques. In an interview which I had with several workers in Cantòn, they told me that planned parenthood required continued and sustained educational work because *the problem was not the young couple, but the mothers-in-law, the grandmothers-to-be*. Since in China families still consist of three generations, the words of the older members still had a great deal of weight.

In 1965 the policy of planned parenthood was to become a reality in China's countryside.

By then Chairman Mao had issued his great call to doctors and medical personnel to centre their work on the countryside. By then the movement for socialist education in the countryside (which later was to take on an enormous amplitude in the Cultural Revolution) had begun to sift again many problems.

It was during the Cultural Revolution, and especially in the last three years, (1968, 1969, 1970), with Chairman Mao's great call for preventive medicine, for the development of medicine in the countryside, for education in medical knowledge, not of a small élite, but of every man, woman and child; with the development in every commune of self-reliance in medical care; with the creation of the barefoot doctor; with the sending of the staffs of city hospitals to the countryside, that planned parenthood took an enormous expansion.

Family planning for the masses

Family planning, in that context, was to be a decision of the masses, and follow the mass line as all other aspects of the construction of socialism in China. Only through total mass participation and involvement, which meant, therefore, through knowledge and decision-making on the part of the masses, could this problem be solved. And it is in this way that family planning is now developing.

In every commune I visited in 1969, at the level of the brigade, family planning was available in the form of the oral pill, also in the form of intra-uterine devices. More were available, of course, through the clinics and hospitals which kept in liaison, through medical teams, with the whole grass-roots network. *The first prerequisite, which is the spontaneous demand of couples for planned parenthood, is now in process of being established throughout China, rural as well as urban.*

In a textile factory I visited in Soochow, 80 per cent of the workers were women; the pill was available to them free of charge; there was no coercion. It would be difficult to find female workers in China who would not agree that two or at the most three children are enough.

Liberation of women

Infant mortality has gone down so dramatically, and the liberation of woman has so drastically altered her status, that most women want to participate in productive work, and not one wishes to have more than two or three healthy children. Chinese women consider it their right to discuss and agree with their husbands on how many children they will have before marriage. I have met and talked with many women, workers, taxi drivers, students, and younger peasant girls; they all felt that it was perfectly natural when considering marriage, to decide, with their consort, this important point of bringing up a family. This is a great transformation from the reticence of the past.

The intra-uterine device is probably still the most commonly used, either the intra-uterine ring, or another type, called 'flower', and in plastic, devised and made in China, and which does not drop out so easily. In the countryside women doing manual labour found that a high proportion of intra-uterine devices dropped out (up to 60 per cent of dropouts occur in India)—hence the modification of the shape of the intra-uterine device in China. The oral pill is well accepted, but there are careful checks, lest there should be some untoward responses. One woman secretary in a revolutionary committee in a factory told me there were some difficulties with the oral pill in that women workers tended to forget to take it regularly (21 days out of 28 to 30 days).

Another doctor in Harbin told me that the Chinese oral pill is free of harmful side-effects noted in certain other countries because the proportions utilized are different and the chemical formulae are also different.

Family planning is not applied to national minority areas, such as Tibet, Inner Mongolia, Sinkiang, and other areas where national minorities live. This is because these areas and their nationalities were extremely poor, and deprived, resulting in under-population.

Self control and delayed marriage

Besides contraceptive techniques, there is also the moral element of self-control. Socialism implies abnegation, unselfishness, struggling against personal egoism for the common good. This demands a high degree of political consciousness, but only in this way can a new morality be evolved. *It has been enjoined to young people to delay the marriage age; this also is a break with tradition in an Asian country where early marriages used to be the rule.* Delay in the age of marriage (for women, to about 25, for men, later) is not an absolute rule; it is a recommendation. Of course many couples are still young when they marry, but not as young as they used to be. Marriage before the age of 18, which at one time was prevalent, is now unknown. By delaying marriage, and thus reproduction, a better balance can be established for the individual, who has more time to grow and mature, intellectually and physically.

Masses educate themselves

Planned parenthood, therefore, is incorporated into the socialist system in China; it also has had its struggle between two lines to adopt a clear, socialist line, Chairman Mao's line, rather than the capitalist line. The most essential thing about it in China is that it is planned parenthood without fear, without economic pressures. Chairman Mao's great dictum, **'Let the masses educate themselves',** is as true where family planning is concerned as in everything else. Within the next decade China will probably have evolved more types of contraceptive techniques. The continued progress of the Chinese woman of which planned parenthood is a feature, makes it certain that in this particular field, as in others, the Chinese people will be masters of their own destiny.

SOURCE: *Japan Quarterly* (December 1970)

India
The second piece is an account of a pioneering experiment in massive vasectomy which was conducted in the state of Kerala in India. The first camp was held at Cochin, the capital city of Ernakulam district in Kerala State, from 20 November to 20 December, 1970. At this camp 15,005 vasectomies were performed, setting an all-India record. Encouraged by the success of the first camp, the district collector and the family planning bureau organised a second one-month long sterilisation

camp in July 1971 in the same city. At this camp, or 'Family Planning Festival', 62,913 vasectomies and 505 tubectomies were performed, exceeding by more than four times the all-India sterilisation record set by the same district only 7 months earlier. These massive sterilisation camps have been hailed as a tremendous breakthrough in India's family planning effort.

These extracts are from the report of S. Krishna Kumar, IAS, who was the district collector of Ernakulam District, Kerala State.

9A S Krishna Kumar
VASECTOMY IN INDIA

The Ernakulam camps set a world record in vasectomies performed for a given population group in a given length of time. Of the 78,423 acceptors sterilized in the two camps, 34,481 were residents of Ernakulam District, and they constituted 11·5 percent of the 300,000 couples eligible for family planning in the district. Coupling the achievements of the camps with prior program performance an estimated 29 percent of Ernakulam District's eligible couples are currently protected by a family planning method. This includes 38·1 percent of couples in the district with three or more children who have now been provided permanent contraceptive protection.

In spite of the short duration of the motivational effort and the massive nature of the camps, the distribution of acceptors by age of husband, age of wife, parity, income, educational status, religious composition, and rural and urban residence is roughly the same as in the normal program of the district, the state, and the country. Also in spite of the higher incentives given to the acceptors and promoters of sterilization at the camps —four to five times the normal—the total cost per birth prevented has been roughly the same as for the normal program.

The camps demonstrate that large masses of people can be motivated to accept sterilization in a short span of time by an organized and concentrated effort. They provide a spectacular example of a family planning program transcending the traditional health and family planning network to become a total community effort.

Background
ERNAKULAM DISTRICT

Ernakulam, one of ten districts in the state of Kerala, forms the geographic, commercial, and industrial center of the state. The headquarters of the district is Cochin City, Kerala's only major all-weather port and the fifth largest port in India. The district has a total population of 2·38 million (1971 census)—11 percent of the state's population and 0·4 percent of the Indian population. It has a population density of 727 persons per square kilometer.

The literacy rate of 65·3 percent in Ernakulam is higher than the literacy rates of Kerala State (60·2 per cent) and India (29·3 percent). Compared with 16·3 percent in Kerala State and 19·9 percent in India, 27·6 percent of the district's population resides in urban areas. Ernakulam has 985 females per 1,000 males compared with 1,019 in Kerala, and 932 in the country. Ernakulam District's decennial population growth of 27·36 percent during 1961–1971 was greater than the comparable figures of 25·89 percent in Kerala and 24·66 percent in India. There are an estimated 300,000 currently married couples with wives in the reproductive age groups in Ernakulam District, including couples who have already accepted contraceptive services through the family planning program.

ORIGIN OF THE EXPERIMENT

A District Development Seminar was organized at Cochin in August 1970 to devise an overall strategy for the future development of Ernakulam District and to lay the blueprint of a District Development Master Plan containing a multi-pronged development program. In the overall development strategy, limitation of population growth was given the highest priority. The district therefore set itself the ambitious target of bringing its entire 300,000 eligible couples into the program within five

THE DEVELOPING WORLD 83

years. This was to be achieved through a program involving the active participation of the entire community.

To focus public attention on the population issue and to provide a rallying point for a popular movement, massive family planning camps, organized as festivals, were visualized as the first step in the district's intensive drive. Sterilization was to be popularized at these camps in order to create immediate and substantial demographic impact. Vasectomy was chosen because the operation is easy to perform at low cost and requires little time and no hospitalization; thus, it was deemed best suited for the massive camp approach. The District Family Planning Bureau, under the guidance of the collector, organized publicity and field work. Intensive publicity and educational activities began two weeks before the camp, building momentum up to the time the camp opened. The publicity at the block level was through public meetings, attended by 2,000 to 3,000 people and through group talks for audiences of less than 100 persons. Frequent press releases were issued at the district level appealing for popular participation in the program. All-India Radio Stations in Kerala cooperated with frequent announcements. In rural areas, street corner meetings, loudspeaker announcements, wall posters, bit notices, banners, slides at all local theatres, variety entertainments, and cultural performances on family planning publicized the festival at Cochin. The field publicity units, the health education units, and the film units of the District Family Planning Bureau concentrated on the camps.

Lists of eligible couples with their addresses, data on age of husband and wife and the number of children were prepared for each local area by the family planning workers. Couples in the reproductive age group with two or more living children were eligible for sterilization. House-to-house campaigns and squad work by teams of family planning educators and public workers were organized in each panchayat.

The camp was held at Cochin's town hall, a large auditorium

with an extensive compound. The entire compound was covered with rain-proof coverings and the front of the premises was adorned with an architectural facade. The festival premises were attractively decorated and illuminated. Inside the auditorium 50 white painted hardboard cubicles with operation tables and accessories were set up. Arrangements were made at the festival site for reception of the acceptors, registration, medical checkup, preoperative preparation, laboratory examination, operation theaters with cubicles and medication sections. Also provided were free coffee stalls and free canteens, counters for issue of incentive money, distribution of condoms, research and study sections, and an entertainment auditorium where variety shows were performed 24 hours a day. The layout was designed to ensure a smooth flow of acceptors through the various medical and nonmedical sections in an uninterrupted and orderly manner without confusion or inconvenience to either staff or acceptors. An average of 2,000 acceptors could be served every day in the July camp with the figure rising to 3,000 on certain days. An audiovisual exhibition on family planning was organized at the festival premises to coincide with each one-month-long camp. Public functions occurred at the inauguration and conclusion of the festival and also at intervals when the camps were in progress. Baby shows were organized at the camps to project the image of family planning with special reference to maternal and child health and to focus public attention on prenatal, natal, and postnatal pediatric services. Only the babies of parents adopting permanent methods of contraception were allowed to participate in these contests. The festival was visited by cabinet ministers and other dignitaries from the government of India, the chief minister and ministers of the state government, and eminent economists and representatives of national and international organisations concerned with the family planning program.

INCENTIVES

Large incentives played an important role in motivating many acceptors, especially from the lower income strata. Incentives to acceptors of vasectomy or tubectomy in the July camp were as follows:

	Male Rs.	Female Rs.
Compensation amount as per usual central government rate	21·00	29·00
Special Government of India grant	14·10	14·10
Payment by local self government body such as Corporation of Cochin, municipalities and panchayats	10·00	10·00
One week's free ration for the family of the individual (specially sanctioned by the state government)	14·00	14·00
CARE gift kit containing 3 kgs. of rice, one saree and one dhothi (Contribution of CARE)	40·00	40·00
Value of lottery ticket (Prize money divided by the number of acceptors—*Government of India funds)	0·40	0·40
Free food at the camp site (met from special Government of India grant)	1·50	1·50
Total	101·00	109·00
Free transport to and from the camp (average in terms of bus fare)	6·00	6·00
Medicines in connection with the operation	7·00	20·00
Total	13·00	26·00
Grand total in cash, kind, and services	114·00	135·00

Promoters received, in addition to the usual rate of Rs. 2 sanctioned by the government, Rs. 8 from CARE, making a total of Rs. 10 for each promoter.

* A total of Rs. 26,200 was distributed to 101 prize winners of the lottery conducted for acceptors of sterilization at the festival. The first prize was Rs. 10,000 and the other prizes were: 3 prizes of Rs. 1000 each, 5 prizes of Rs. 500 each, 10 prizes of Rs. 250 each and 82 prizes of Rs. 100 each.

Suitable incentives for the project staff and field workers in the form of monetary and other awards were announced by the district collector before the beginning of the drive. They included special merit certificates from the government for officials and nonofficials performing outstanding service in connection with this intensive drive; special monetary awards for field workers for maximum promotional effort; and awards to institutions and panchayats sending the maximum number of persons to the camp. In each category of officials and nonofficials connected with the organization and conduct of the camp the best persons in terms of meritorious services rendered were recognized and rewarded. The project staff other than those compensated by government as per rules on a per operation basis (doctors, nurses, and so on) were given a daily project allowance as a token compensation for the arduous nature of their work.

The camps succeeded in large measure in overcoming the resistance of the individual to vasectomy arising from embarrassment, fear of others knowing about the operation, and prudery regarding a subject relating to sex and reproduction. It was with the aim of breaking down this barrier that the town hall at the very center of the city was selected as the location for the camps, and they were organized in the full public gaze. The image of family planning as a clinical program was radically altered by the festive atmosphere of the camps. The town hall resembled more than anything else a center of popular activities.

During the month-long festivals the gaily decorated premises were alive with a constant flux of people arriving from the various parts of the district and state; long queues; doctors, nurses, and officials busily going about their jobs; the public address system filling the air with directions and messages; government and private requisitioned vehicles clogging traffic around the camp site; and the huge crowds viewing the entertainment programs. Decorations, banners, exhibitions, the permanent theater for music, puppet shows, films, dance dramas, programs by the state's leading literary figures, and other cultural entertainments twenty-four hours a day, processions, decorated floats, baby shows with prizes for healthy babies of sterilized parents, the lottery, and the attractive gifts combined to create the aura of the traditional Indian festival—a successful medium for any campaign strategy.

An illuminated signboard on the front facade of the festival building prominently displayed up-to-date figures of the total number of operations performed at the camp, and the score was a focus of interest to every person passing the festival site. Highlights of the camp and the daily number of sterilizations performed were also given extensive publicity through newspapers, local stations of the All-India Radio, loudspeaker announcements, and notices.

Throughout the district, family planning vehicles could be seen with their loads of acceptors going to and from the camp. Acceptors returning to other districts with the colourful CARE bags of incentives were a constant sight in the state bus and train services.

Conclusion

The development of national family planning programs is a truly historic innovation of recent times and its impact is still not fully measured. India was the first country to officially recognize the need for population limitation as an integral part of its development plans. The success of the national program in India is a crucial variant between prosperity and poverty, nonhunger and hunger, progress and stagnation, stability and instability, and fulfillment and nonfulfillment of this nation's rightful destiny. The task of bringing the country's birth rate to the desired level is enormous and complex and it is not likely that one contraceptive method or one managerial technique will serve a population as vast and diverse as that of India. But the Ernakulam experiment goes to show that with a combination of dedicated and dynamic leadership at all levels, improvement in service, efficient functioning of staff, effective supervision and guidance to workers, intensive propaganda and educational effort, prompt attention in cases of complaints, active involvement of nonofficials and the community at large, concurrent appraisal and better feedback arrangements, appropriate inputs, and above all imaginative planning, organization and management, it is possible to motivate large masses of people to accept family planning in a very short span of time. The pioneering effort at Ernakulam has now been duplicated quite successfully in various parts of the country.

SOURCE: Population Council of New York, *Studies in Family Planning* (August 1972)

Here are a quotation from Mrs Gandhi and some official policy statements made by the Indian Government on the question of population.

We must ensure that every child in every home is a wanted child and has his rightful share of health, education and employment.

Family planning, therefore, is at the base of our whole behaviour of national development.

SOURCE: Statement made by Indira Gandhi, Prime Minister of India

9B Government of India
INDIAN FAMILY PLANNING

First five-year plan, 1951–6
Policy
The rapid increase in population and the consequent pressure on the limited resources available have brought to the forefront the urgency of problems of family planning. The main appeal for family planning is, however, based on considerations of the health and welfare of the family. Family limitation or the spacing of the children is necessary and desirable in order to secure better health for the mother and better care and up-

THE DEVELOPING WORLD 89

bringing of the children. Measures directed to this end, therefore, form part of the public health programme.*

Second five-year plan, 1956–61
Policy
The problem of regulating India's population from the dual standpoint of size and quality is of the utmost importance to national welfare and national planning.

The family planning programme was primarily directed to the building up of an active public opinion in favour of family planning and the promotion of family planning advice and service on the basis of existing knowledge. At the same time demographic as well as medical and biological studies were taken up. It is proposed to develop this programme further during the second plan.†

Third five-year plan, 1961–6
Policy
In the Chapter on Long-Term Economic Development, certain provisional estimates of increase in population over the next fifteen years have been cited, and it has been stated that the objective of stabilizing the growth of population over a reasonable period must be at the very centre of planned development. In this context, the greatest stress has to be placed in the third and subsequent Five-Year Plans on the programme of family planning. This will involve intensive education, provision of facilities and advice on the largest scale possible and widespread popular effort in every rural and urban community. In the circumstances of the country, family planning has to be undertaken, not merely as a major development programme, but as a nation-wide movement which embodies a basic attitude towards a better life for the individual, the family and the community.‡

* Government of India, *First Five Year Plan* (Delhi, 1953), 218
† Government of India, *Second Five Year Plan* (Delhi, 1956), 553
‡ Government of India, *Third Five Year Plan* (Delhi, 1961), 675

India's objective of attaining socio-economic betterment of the people can only be fulfilled if the rate of growth of population is controlled and human skill and resources are developed to the desired extent. The government of India have recognised family planning as a key programme for the success of the country's Five Year Plans of development and have adopted a nation-wide programme with the objective of reducing the birth rate from 40 per thousand at present to 25 per thousand as expeditiously as possible. The operational goal for achieving this objective is to create facilities for 90 per cent of the married population of India, for the adoption of family planning by:
  (i) Group acceptance of a small size family;
  (ii) Personal knowledge about family planning methods; and
  (iii) Ready availability of supplies and services.*

* Government of India Planning Commission, *Fourth Five Year Plan—A draft outline* (Delhi, no date), 346.

SOURCE: United Nations Population Division

AFRICA

Government attitudes are more diverse in Africa. Although at least six governments have committed themselves, according to UN figures, to national programmes that promote fertility reduction, there are some African countries in which no governmental attitude can be detected and others in which, rather than favouring fertility reduction, the desire for continuing and rapid population growth has been expressed.

There follow extracts from official Botswanan, Ghanaian and Kenyan statements, an article by Dr Francis Olu Okediji, Associate Professor in the Department of Sociology at Ibadan University, Nigeria, and, finally, transcripts of programmes on family planning appearing in 'Radio Magazine' on Tanzania Radio, and on Uganda Radio.

10A Government of Botswana
FAMILY PLANNING POLICY

A start has been made in initiating family planning with the assistance of the International Planned Parenthood Federation.

SOURCE: International Conference of Ministers Responsible for Social Welfare, statement prepared by governments, United Nations document, E/CONF 55/7, Add 1 (July 1968), 12

As far as Government is concerned, there is not the slightest intention to impose family planning on anyone, but merely to make the advantages of family planning available to the population. The Government adheres strongly to the view that the size of an individual's family is entirely his own affair and Government does not intend interfering with the personal rights of any individual.

SOURCE: Letter from the Ministry of Education, Health and Labour, Republic of Botswana (June 1969)

10B Republic of Ghana
FAMILY PLANNING POLICY

Estimates based on 1960 data indicate that with unrestricted immigration and no decline in fertility, Ghana's population could be expected to increase to over 17 million by 1985 and to about 32 million by the year 2,000, which is only 32 years away. It is clear that the economy will not easily be expanded to accommodate at a rising level of living the additional millions that will be added in the next few years. Nor the future millions that would come with greater and greater rapidity in ensuing years.

. . . with the conviction that present rates of population growth are detrimental to individual and family welfare and constitute major hindrances to the attainment of development objectives, the government believes that voluntary planning of the size of families and reductions in the rates of population growth are in the vital interest of the nation and proposes that a national policy be adopted to advance these interests.

SOURCE: Republic of Ghana, *Population Planning for National*

Progress and Prosperity—Ghana Population Policy (March 1969), 8

10C Republic of Kenya
FAMILY PLANNING POLICY

1 African Socialism and its application to Kenya
Policy
The Government's capacity to achieve its desired objectives is restricted by our limited resources, which restrain our ability to expand, and by our high rate of population growth, which rapidly increases the size of the task. With population growing in excess of 3 per cent per annum nearly seven million jobs will be needed by the year 2000 and over 230,000 adult males will at that time be added to the labour force each year. A more moderate rate of population growth of 1·7 per cent per annum, approximating the world rate, would mean a male labour force of 4·5 million growing at 60,000 per annum in the year 2000. The effect of slower growth on numbers of children of primary school age is even more pronounced. With present fertility rates universal education would require facilities for over six million children in the year 2000 at an annual recurrent cost of perhaps £49 million. More moderate growth would reduce this cost to £18 million because facilities would be needed for only 2·3 million children.

SOURCE: Republic of Kenya, *African Socialism and its Application to Planning in Kenya* (1965), 31

2 Development plan, 1966-70
Policy
Data from the recent demographic inquiry covering 10 per cent of the population suggest that on the average between seven and eight children are born to women reaching the age of 50.

At present the population of Kenya increases by about 3 per cent each year, and if the habit of the families to have many children does not change this rate of growth will increase to 4 per cent in a few years time. The population problem has such a serious impact on the future development of the country that the Government has decided to place strong emphasis on measures to promote family planning education.

SOURCE: Republic of Kenya, *Development Plan 1966–1970* (1966), 51–5

Dr Okediji's article ran as follows.

11 Dr Francis Olu Okediji
SOCIOLOGICAL BACKGROUND TO FAMILY LIFE IN TROPICAL AFRICA

The family, whatever its form, is usually part of a larger kinship system: the family is an embodiment of rules which govern the relationship between the husband and wife or wives. Two types of family can be distinguished in African societies: the nuclear family and the extended family.

A nuclear family consists of father, mother and children. The extended family embraces a web of inter-related lineages involving several nuclear families, all associating through occasional family meetings, ceremonies, rituals and seasonal festivals. Members of the extended family are bound together by strong social bonds and the extended family performs social, economic, religious and political functions for its members.

There is general agreement that traditional African societies, which are organized predominantly around the extended family system, are characterized by high fertility levels as all pre-industrial societies throughout history. Two types of explanation are usually given for this demographic fact:

1 from the society's point of view, high fertility is a functional adjustment to the high mortality existing in such societies

2 from the point of view of the reproducing couple, high fer-

tility is motivated by the following factors: the economic value of children, the prestige which is derived by parents from the numerical strength of their children; the assistance which offspring give their parents during sickness and old age, the desire for more male children, especially in patrilineal societies where descent and property are traced through the male line.

In Western Europe, forces combined to bring about the evolution of the nuclear family. The needs and influences of the pre-industrial society were slowly undermined, and the extended family system broke up fairly easily, since European societies always had a tradition of simpler kinship structures. Today, however, developing countries have suddenly been provided with modern plants and factories which require comparatively little in the way of individual skills, and this indicates that a repetition of the Western European pattern should not necessarily be anticipated. The empirical evidence from tropical Africa which confirms this argument includes studies which show how the extended family system has persisted in cities such as Brazzaville, Dakar, Lagos, Ibadan, Leopoldville and Stanleyville. This survival of the extended family system can be explained by the various services (such as recreational, religious, economic, legal and political) which it performs for urban dwellers, for whom social welfare programmes are non-existent.

Belief is an important variable which is related to attitudes towards family planning. Among the Yoruba of Western Nigeria, for example, it is widely believed among illiterate families that sexual intercourse during the period of lactation can poison the child. It is because of this that the traditional two-year period of nursing is common among illiterate Yoruba women. Another traditional belief found among Yoruba parents, is that sexual intercourse during the period of menstruation leads to the birth of an albino child. Some religions, such as Islam and Catholicism, appear to frown upon the use of contraception for pregnancy control. The influence of education appears to weaken strict adherence to these religions with regard to pregnancy control. More systematic research, however, is needed in African societies to probe the dynamics of the relationship between religion and fertility control.

Rural and urban differences

There are numerous factors which tend to perpetuate high fertility levels in rural areas, in tropical Africa. The average age at marriage for females is about fifteen, and the anticipated decline in mortality, due to improvements in medical facilities, means that more women than ever before will be living through the reproductive years. As already cited, social and religious forces result in high value being placed on numerous offspring. Widespread illiteracy, and the low proportion of women with secondary and tertiary education, militate against any change in attitude towards the practice of family planning. It seems unrealistic to expect strong motivation for family planning to develop in the rural areas, or in the traditional-rural sectors of urban areas in tropical Africa, without the socio-cultural changes which will place economic and social sanctions on raising large families.

It is anticipated therefore, because of the Western European demographic experience, that as a society undergoes transformation from rural to urban, the social and economic penalties of raising large families will be more greatly felt, and consequently there will be a greater desire to limit family size to avoid these penalties.

As far as most nations in tropical Africa are concerned there is so far only a little empirical evidence showing any significant decline in the importance attached to large families, as only a few studies have been done. However, all studies undertaken so far indicate a decline in the importance attached to large families as societies change from rural to urban. For example: in Ghana, there is evidence of a difference between urban and rural residents in the ideal number of children they want. Birth rates in Ghana seem to be about one-tenth lower in urban areas than in the surrounding rural villages. Among the urban elite families in Ghana, there is a tendency to consider more than four children somewhat excessive. In Nigeria, there appears to be a declining trend in the desire for large families in urban areas like Ibadan and Lagos. In Kenya, and in the cities of Ibadan and Lagos in Nigeria, and among the urban elite in Ghana, there is widespread knowledge of some methods of family planning.

Rural-urban differences in the control of fertility and attitudes towards family planning can be summarized as follows: the various indicators of potential fertility control were at their lowest intensity in predominant traditional areas characterized by a subsistence economy. However, these indicators rose with transition to cash cropping areas, and further still in rural areas characterized by commercial activities. This change tends to be even more remarkable, in larger towns where family planning clinics are available.

One last important point ought to be made. The enthusiasm of developed nations for financing and organizing family planning clinics in so many of the nations of the 'third world', can easily be misconstrued as a political gimmick to control the population of the latter, unless economic arrangements with these developing nations stand scrutiny as being fair and liberal.

SOURCE: IPPF: Communicating family planning

The radio transcripts from Tanzania and Uganda are as follows:

12A Tanzania Radio
FAMILY PLANNING PROGRAMME

Time: 10 minutes

Sound effects: Introductory music; conversation of women in a clinic waiting room

Announcer: Good evening, Ladies and Gentlemen. Tonight Radio Magazine will take you to a Family Planning Clinic. Earlier today we visited the Amtullabai Karimjee Clinic at Mnazi Mmoja in Dar es Salaam to talk to some of the ladies there about what they think of family planning. We were received by Family Planning Health Educator, Mrs. Akim, who introduced us to some of the attending patients.

Health Educator: Good afternoon, ladies. Let me introduce Mr. Halimoja, who has come from Radio Tanzania to ask us a few questions about family planning. Welcome, Mr. Halijoma.

Announcer: Thank you, Mrs. Akim, and Good afternoon, ladies. What is your name, Mama?

Patient No. 1: Mama Hadija.

Announcer: Mama Hadija, I didn't know that such a place as this existed. How did you hear about it?

Patient No. 1: I heard about it from Mama Mandeleo when she came to the Clinic.

Announcer: And which clinic was that?

Patient No. 1: Magomeni Clinic, when I took my child for vaccination.

Announcer: How do you think family planning will help you?

Patient No. 1: Family planning will give me a rest. In the last three years I have had three babies and I haven't had time to look after them properly.

Announcer: How long do you want to rest before having another baby?

D

Patient No. 1: I haven't decided yet—probably two or three years.

Announcer: Thank you, Mama Hadija. And now, Mama, what is your name?

Patient No. 2: Mama Pili.

Announcer: Can you tell our radio listeners why you like family planning?

Patient No. 2: I have been coming to the family planning clinic for about five years now. Family planning has made it possible for my husband and me to have our babies when we wanted them. I am stronger, my children are healthier, and my home is happier because of this good service.

Announcer: Thank you, Mama Pili. I hope you have been able to tell your friends about this. And now, this lady here—what is your name, Mama?

Patient No. 3: Mama Fatuma.

Announcer: Where are you from, Mama Fatuma?

Patient No. 3: From Yombo.

Announcer: Ah yes, and have you come for the same purpose as these other ladies?

Patient No. 3: I was referred by the doctor at the hospital. I have been ill for a long time and he told me that another pregnancy while I am recovering would be dangerous.

Announcer: Well, thank you, Mrs Akim, for making this interview possible and thank you, ladies, for being so helpful.

SOURCE: Tanzania Radio—'Radio Magazine'.

12B Uganda Radio
FAMILY PLANNING PROGRAMME

Audience: Women of child-bearing years

Time: 30 seconds

First woman: What are you all doing here?

Second woman: Mrs. Rubongoya is in bed; she had a baby boy last year but now she is expecting again!

First woman: Where is Mr. Rubongoya? I hear they have several children. Edith has six and Mary has five.

Effects: Children cry and fight for matoke.

First woman: Please go and see the children, why are they fighting?

Second woman: I cannot make those children keep quiet, not even stop them from fighting. They are hungry because the matoke was not enough.

First woman: All right, go to my house and bring some meat and beans.

Edith: How long are you going to help us? You are not going to bring us some food every day. Who can help us best?

First woman: Go to the Family Planning Association for advice.

SOURCE: Uganda Radio.

LATIN AMERICA

In many Latin American countries population is growing at rates that are among the highest in the world. In several of these countries the governments have been concerned with the high frequency of illegal abortion, which has become an important social and health problem, and therefore favour family planning as a defence against abortion. In Chile, for example, there was one illegal abortion for every three births, which not only jeopardised women's health but also overburdened the health services.

A key event was the meeting on Population Policies in Relation to Development in Latin America, which was held in Caracas, Venezuela, 11–16 September 1967, under the joint sponsorship of the Organisation of American States (OAS), the Pan American Health Organisation (PAHO), the Population Council and the Aspen Institute for Humanistic Studies, with the cooperation of the government of Venezuela. The meeting was attended by ministers and other high officials from planning, health, education, labour and urban and rural development agencies in the member states of the OAS, as well as by experts from both public and private, national and international, institutions concerned with population and development questions in Latin America—a total of nearly 200 people.

Among other things, the meeting, in its Declaration, noted the impact of high fertility on the health of Latin American women as well as a more favourable religious climate towards birth control.

13 Caracas Meeting on Population Policies
DECLARATION

The high fertility of Latin American women—verified in recent surveys—causes serious dangers to health that are translated into a high rate of induced abortion, among other consequences. Abortion is one of the main causes of maternal illness, disability, and death in Latin America. High fertility also aggravates the prevailing conditions of infant malnutrition. In addition, it may entail social and economic problems, among them family breakdown, desertion of the home by the man, juvenile delinquency, and other social maladjustments. From the medical standpoint, moreover, the spacing and limitation of pregnancies makes it possible to improve the health conditions of the mother and of children already born.

Therefore, and in response to the demand for information and services already evident in Latin America and to the right of the married couple to decide on the number and spacing of children, it is considered that the public, private, and social-security health systems should be equipped to put the information and medical assistance required for family planning within the reach of persons of all social levels. For this, as action programs are planned and carried out, it will be necessary to improve the training of medical and paramedical personnel in the biology and physiology of reproduction and in the demographic, socioeconomic, and health aspects of family planning. Special efforts should be made to acquaint illiterate people with the existence of family-planning methods.

In the consideration of these problems, the rural population, which is still unreached by health services, deserves attention at least equal to that given to the urban sector.

For family well-being in its true sense and real community action for its improvement, the efforts of programs in health, infant care and nutrition, maternal welfare, social security, and family planning must be coordinated.

From the standpoint of the health sector itself and of development programs as a whole, there should be periodic evaluation of the scope and intensity of health programs and their effect on the basic demographic variables.

In relation to family planning, it is important to note that the new trends in religious circles reveal a growing acceptance of programs that, with full respect for the individual conscience and for the various creeds, put the information and services necessary for a free decision on family size within the reach of the population. These circles also mention the emphasis that should be placed on socioreligious values such as the indissolubility of the family, conjugal love, and responsible parenthood.

The meeting went on to make five general recommendations. In Latin America perhaps more than in any other region in the world there is a fear that international assistance for population and family planning programmes may be seen as a substitute for development aid and better terms of trade, rather than being complementary to it.

Caracas Meeting on Population Policies GENERAL RECOMMENDATIONS

1. That the Latin American governments, the private sector, university institutions, public information media, and public and private international organizations promote the broadest possible review and study of population problems within the context of economic and social development trends and policies, taking into account the complex interrelationship between population growth and other aspects of social evolution and change in Latin America.

2. That the action programs already under way in any field affecting the demographic variables—whether in health and family planning, education, the labour force, agricultural development, regional or urban development, or any other—be evaluated periodically in terms of the general criteria and propositions adopted at the present Meeting, in order that they may be adjusted to the objectives of the population policies within the framework of the plans, programs, and activities designed to accelerate economic and social development and to take full advantage of material and human resources to the benefit of the Latin American peoples.

3. That in their national economic and social development plans the governments take into proper consideration and include—as variables, not as fixed data—the factors related to population dynamics and its impact on the achievement of the general and sectoral goals, and also the inter-relationships between the growth and changing characteristics of the

population and the growth and structural change of the economy.

4. That, since the expected results of the plans and programs of the Latin American countries for economic and social development are subject in large part to the contingencies of international economic and financial cooperation and to changes and fluctuations in world markets, with a consequent effect on the incomes received by the Latin American population, the governments intensify their collective and individual efforts, through the appropriate international organizations, to ensure the backing and action necessary for expanding their foreign trade, within the Latin American region and outside, and reducing market instability.

5. That in the processes of Latin American economic integration due attention be directed toward the influence of demographic phenomena on the capacity of the participating countries to orient the development of their economies in a way compatible with the integration commitments, and especially toward problems of scale and purchasing power of markets.

SOURCE: Report of Caracas Meeting, 1967

Finally, here are statements from two South American leaders.

14 Former Presidents Camargo and Frei
STATEMENTS

Can the headlong multiplication of the poorer, uneducated, and helpless populations be allowed to set the stage for a crisis of incalculable proportions? Can the hunger that prevails among broad sectors of the earth's population be tolerated? Is there any possibility of producing, processing, and distributing the food that will be needed by the population that the earth is expected to have in 10 years, in 20 years, or by the end of the century?

The issue is simply to know whether we can stand, and to what point we can stand the pressure of a growing population on earth.

SOURCE: Statements by Alberto Lleras Camargo, former president of Colombia

The population explosion is a problem that cannot be evaded. It is necessary not only to study it but to work out solutions and face up to it with courage. This is a problem affecting not just each family and each country, but all humanity.

SOURCE: Eduardo Frei, former president, Republic of Chile

PART THREE

The Developed World

The United Nations summarises the position in the developed world as follows.

15 UN
THE DEVELOPED WORLD IN 1970

A diversity of official positions concerning matters of family planning can also be discerned among the more developed countries. In these countries, social considerations are most in evidence. Rarely is it argued at the present time that an unduly high or low rate of population growth depresses economic conditions in one of the more developed countries. Inasmuch as the social problems differ, in a few of the more developed countries, couples with small families are encouraged to have more children; in other countries the facilitation of fertility reduction is promoted; and there are also some countries where measures of both types exist at the same time, responding to a diversity of social needs, without constituting a contradiction in general policy.

Japan, the USSR and various Eastern European and Scandinavian countries have been prominent in connexion with government policies facilitating access to clinically performed abortions. In some instances this is evidently designed as a temporizing policy, pending the wider popular spread of contraceptive methods. In a few instances, however, as in Bulgaria, Hungary and Romania, where the birth rate has fallen unusually low, new measures have been adopted to counteract the limitation of family size which is believed to be excessive.

In some countries, for example the United Kingdom, the United States and Yugoslavia, enactments have been designed so that means of contraception shall not be lacking to any families desiring them, whatever their social stratum. In several other countries like Canada and France, some old laws concerning the distribution of contraceptive devices, which have long been circumvented in various ways, have been abrogated. But in some of them no legal concessions have as yet been made to the tendency in many developed countries towards individualism in matters relating to human reproduction. In many of the economically more developed countries subsidies exist in various forms, whether as a scheme of family allowances, tax exemptions, educational or housing assistance, or other provisions, to encourage families of limited means to have at least the desired numbers of children. Sensitive to changing pressures arising from social requirements, Governments of some of these countries modify the details of legislation in these several respects with greater or lesser frequency.

SOURCE: UN, *A Concise Summary of the World Population Situation in 1970*

BRITAIN
There are signs of growing recognition in certain developed countries of the urgency of their population problems. In May 1971 the report of a House of Commons Select Committee began by citing the latest demographic statistics.

16 House of Commons Select Committee on Science and Technology
REPORT

The estimated home population of the United Kingdom in June 1970 was 55,711,000. The total for England and Wales was

48,988,000 of whom 35·3 per cent. or 17,316,000 lived in the South East of England. The highest concentrations of people were formed by the 6,789,000 who lived in the North-West at a density of 3·44 to the acre and by those in the South-East at a density of 2·56 to the acre. These figures may be compared with a density of 1·27 persons to the acre in the Netherlands in 1969 and 1·28 in Belgium. The lowest concentrations of population in England and Wales were in Wales with 2,734,000 persons at 0·53 to the acre, and in East Anglia with 1,673,000 at 0·54 to the acre. The population of Scotland at the same date was 5,199,000 giving a density of 0·27 to the acre and that of Northern Ireland was 1,524,000 at a density of 0·44 to the acre.

Over twenty-one years have elapsed since the Report of the Royal Commission on Population was published. The Commission was set up in 1944 largely because of fears of a falling population. One of their main conclusions was that 'total numbers will continue to grow in the near future, perhaps even for another generation. The growth will not be rapid and the further addition to the population which can be expected is not large.' They considered that a replacement size of family was desirable in Britain at that time. They were convinced that policy could not be 'neutral' in this matter since in many ways policy and administration had a continuing influence on the trend of family size.

The Royal Commission recognised that the population problem would always be changing and that this would require continuous study. They recommended that the Lord President of the Council, who at that time had responsibility for scientific matters, should be made responsible for a continuous watch over population movements and their bearing on national policies. He never assumed this duty nor has any specific allocation of it been made to Ministers.

In the background the Registrar General and the Government Actuary have maintained a continuing review of population trends. Despite the failure until recently to implement the Royal Commission's recommendations on the expansion of the General Register Office, their surveillance has disclosed remarkable changes from the assumptions made by the Royal Commission.

It will be clear from the facts we have already cited in this Report that we are now faced with the problem of a rapidly rising population and not with fears of a declining one. In the words of Sir Solly Zuckerman, then Chief Scientific Adviser to the Government, 'the basic fact is that in the remaining 30 years of this century provision may have to be made for almost as many additional people as have been accommodated in the first 70 years of the century'. Although the Royal Commission made a variety of calculations on the future size of population they assumed that the population at the end of the century would be of the order of 54 million. Recent calculations by the Government Actuary's Department and the General Register Office illustrate the extent to which unforeseen changes in marriage patterns and a rise in birth rate have affected population projections.

Base year for projection	Actual population in each year (millions)	Projected future population of U.K. in years (millions)		
		1980	1990	2000
1960	52·6	57·7	60·6	63·8
1961	52·9	60·1	63·6	67·5
1962	53·4	60·6	65·2	71·1
1963	53·8	60·7	65·4	71·6
1964	54·2	61·4	67·0	74·7
1965	54·5	61·2	66·8	74·6
1966	54·8	60·0	65·1	72·1
1967	55·1	59·5	64·2	70·3
1968	55·4	59·3	63·2	68·2
1969	55·6	58·6	62·0	66·1

Projections must be used with care. Professor Glass considered the official projections unrealistic beyond the short term since they made assumptions about future marriage habits and family size (Q. 758–65). 'Projections are bound to be speculations; as such they must be treated with caution'. Dr. Benjamin of the Social Science Research Council said that a projection was not a forecast; it was merely a way of illustrating the long term effects of present trends (Q. 590). As Sir Solly Zuckerman observed, the actual growth of population has usually been greater than anticipated and where there have been downturns in growth they have been temporary (Q. 110).

Despite margins of error the cardinal fact remains that all recent projections agree on a substantial and continuing increase in population. What is more the limitation of official projections to the year 2000 is arbitrary. Estimates carried forward on the same bases show a continuing growth.

The committee cited the evidence of the Conservation Society.

This evidence should be considered in contrast to the statement of the Conservation Society: 'We have to ask ourselves is Britain likely to be a better place to live in with a steadily growing population or will it be worse? Does life somehow become better when there are more people to experience it or not? The Conservation Society believes that the quality of life is crucially dependent on the amount of land and the pressures upon it, that on this criterion Britain is already overcrowded, and additional numbers can only diminish the quality of life'.

Having considered the evidence, the committee felt justified in drawing the following conclusion:

CONCLUSION
The Government must act to prevent the consequences of population growth becoming intolerable for the every day conditions of life

RECOMMENDATION

We, therefore, recommend setting up, as an integral and permanent part of the machinery of Government, a Special Office directly responsible to the Prime Minister, with the following duties:

(1) To co-ordinate and improve the study of United Kingdom and world population trends, including internal and external migration, and their consequences.
(2) To extend this study to the inter-relation between population and such major issues as food supplies, natural resources, economic growth, and the environment.
(3) To appraise in the context of population policy the plans of the main Departments of State for housing, water supplies, food, transport, fiscal policy, employment, education, health services and other relevant matters.
(4) In the light of these studies and appraisals to advise the Government on population policy.
(5) To publicise the effects of population levels and their consequences, the role of family limitation and socially responsible parenthood.

We consider that the subject of the Report affects the whole of Government. The direct responsibility for carrying out our recommendation should, therefore, rest with the Prime Minister. We ask that he should make an annual Report to Parliament on the work of the Special Office and that parliamentary time be given, annually, for its debate.

SOURCE: House of Commons Select Committee on Science and Technology, *Population and the United Kingdom*

USA

In the United States, in March 1972, the Commission on Population Growth and the American Future published its report. Here is the text of the letter the chairman of the commission, John D. Rockefeller 3rd, sent to the President and Congress of the United States.

17 John D. Rockefeller 3rd
LETTER TO PRESIDENT AND CONGRESS

Commission on Population Growth
and the American Future
726 Jackson Place, N. W.
Washington, D. C. 20506

March 27, 1972

To the President and Congress of the United States:

I have the honor to transmit for your consideration the Final Report, containing the findings and recommendations, of the Commission on Population Growth and the American Future, pursuant to Sec. 8, PL 91-213.

After two years of concentrated effort, we have concluded that, in the long run, no substantial benefits will result from further growth of the Nation's population, rather that the gradual stabilization of our population through voluntary means would contribute significantly to the Nation's ability to solve its problems. We have looked for, and have not found, any convincing economic argument for continued population growth. The health of our country does not depend on it, nor does the vitality of business nor the welfare of the average person.

The recommendations offered by this Commission are directed towards increasing public knowledge of the causes and consequences of population change, facilitating and guiding the processes of population movement, maximizing information about human reproduction and its consequences for the family, and enabling individuals to avoid unwanted fertility.

To these ends we offer this report in the hope that our findings and recommendations will stimulate serious consideration of an issue that is of great consequence to present and future generations.

Respectfully submitted for the Commission,

John D. Rockefeller 3rd
Chairman

The President
The President of the Senate
The Speaker of the House of Representatives

There follows the first chapter of the Final Report. It is one of the more remarkable statements to have been made in recent years, even though certain important recommendations made by the commission—especially those which dealt with abortion—were flatly rejected by the president.

18 Commission on Population Growth and the American Future
PERSPECTIVE ON POPULATION

In the brief history of this nation, we have always assumed that progress and 'the good life' are connected with population growth. In fact, population growth has frequently been regarded as a measure of our progress. If that were ever the case, it is not now. There is hardly any social problem confronting this nation whose solution would be easier if our population were larger. Even now, the dreams of too many Americans are not being realized; others are being fulfilled at too high a cost. Accordingly, this Commission has concluded that our country can no longer afford the uncritical acceptance of the population growth ethic that 'more is better.' And beyond that, after two years of concentrated effort, we have concluded that no substantial benefits would result from continued growth of the nation's population.

The 'population problem' is long run and requires long-run responses. It is not a simple problem. It cannot be encompassed by the slogans of either of the prevalent extremes: the 'more' or the 'bigger the better' attitude on the one hand, or the emergency-crisis response on the other. Neither extreme is accurate nor even helpful.

It is a problem which can be interpreted in many ways. It is the pressure of population reaching out to occupy open spaces and bringing with it a deterioration of the environment. It can be viewed as the effect on natural resources of increased numbers of people in search of a higher standard of living. It is the impact of population fluctuations in both growth and distribution upon the orderly provision of public services. It can be seen as the concentration of people in metropolitan areas and depopulation elsewhere, with all that implies for the quality of life in both places. It is the instability over time of proportions of the young, the elderly, and the productive. For the family and the individual, it is the control over one's life with respect to the reproduction of new life—the formal and informal pronatalist pressures of an outmoded tradition, and the disadvantages of and to the children involved.

Unlike other great public issues in the United States, population lacks the dramatic event—the war, the riot, the calamity—that galvanizes attention and action. It is easily overlooked and neglected. Yet the number of children born now will seriously affect our lives in future decades. This produces a powerful effect in a double sense: Its fluctuations can be strong and not easily changed; and its consequences are important for the welfare of future generations.

There is scarcely a facet of American life that is not involved with the rise and fall of our birth and death rates: the economy, environment, education, health, family life and sexual practices, urban and rural life, governmental effectiveness and political freedoms, religious norms, and secular life styles. If this country is in a crisis of spirit—environmental deterioration, racial antagonisms, the plight of the cities, the international situation—then population is part of that crisis.

Although population change touches all of these areas of our national life and intensifies our problems, such problems will not be solved by demographic means alone. Population policy is no substitute for social, economic, and environmental policy. Successfully addressing population requires that we also address our problems of poverty, of minority and sex discrimination, of careless exploitation of resources, of environmental deterioration, and of spreading suburbs, decaying cities, and wasted countrysides. By the same token, because population is so tightly interwoven with all of these concerns, whatever success we have in resolving these problems will contribute to easing the complex system of pressures that impel population growth.

Consideration of the population issue raises profound questions of what people want, what they need—indeed, what they are for. What does this nation stand for and where is it going? At some point in the future, the finite earth will not satisfactorily accommodate more human beings—nor will the United States. How is a judgment to be made about when that point will be reached? Our answer is that now is the time to confront the question: 'Why more people?' The answer must be given, we believe, in qualitative not quantitative terms.

The United States today is characterized by low population density, considerable open space, a declining birthrate, movement out of the central cities—but that does not eliminate the concern about population. This country, or any country, always has a 'population problem,' in the sense of achieving a proper balance between size, growth, and distribution on the one hand, and, on the other, the quality of life to which every person in this country aspires.

Nor is this country alone in the world, demographically or in any other way. Many other nations are beginning to recognize the importance of population questions. We need to act prudently, understanding that today's decisions on population have effects for generations ahead. Similarly, we need to act responsibly toward other people in the world: This country's needs and wants, given its wealth, may impinge upon the patrimony of other, less fortunate peoples in the decades ahead. The 'population problem' of the developing countries may be more pressing at this time, but in the longer perspective, it is both proper and in our best interest to participate fully in the worldwide search for the good life, which must include the eventual stabilization of our numbers.

A diversity of views

Ultimately, then, we are concerned not with demographic trends alone, but with the effect of these trends on the realization of the values and goals cherished as part of the American tradition and sought after by minorities who also 'want in.'

One of the basic themes underlying our analysis and policy recommendations is the substitution of quality for quantity; that is, we should concern ourselves with improving the quality of life for all Americans rather than merely adding more Americans.

And unfortunately, for many of our citizens that quality of life is still defined only as enough food, clothing, and shelter. All human beings need a sense of their own dignity and worth, a sense of belonging and sharing, and the opportunity to develop their individual potentialities.

But it is far easier to achieve agreement on abstract values than on their meaning or on the strategy to achieve them. Like the American people generally, this Commission has not been able to reach full agreement on the relative importance of different values or on the analysis of how the 'population problem' reflects other conditions and directions of American society.

Three distinct though overlapping approaches have been distinguished. These views differ in their analysis of the nature of the problem and the general priorities of tasks to be accomplished. But, despite the different perspectives from which population is viewed, all of the population policies we shall recommend are consistent with all three positions.

The first perspective acknowledges the benefits to be gained by slowing growth, but regards our population problem today primarily as a result of large numbers of people being unable to control an important part of their lives—the number of children they have. The persistence of this problem reflects an effective denial of freedom of choice and equality of access to the means of fertility control. In this view, the population problem is regarded more as the sum of such individual problems than as a societal problem transcending the interests of individuals; the welfare of individuals and that of the general society are seen as congruent, at least at this point in history. The potential conflict between these two levels is mitigated by the knowledge that freedom from unwanted childbearing would contribute significantly to the stabilization of population.

Reproductive decisions should be freely made in a social context without pronatalist pressures—the heritage of a past when the survival of societies with high mortality required high fertility. The proper mission for government in this matter is to ensure the fullest opportunity for people to decide their own future in this regard, based on the best available knowledge; then the demographic outcome becomes the democratic solution.

Beyond these goals, this approach depends on the processes of education, research, and national debate to illuminate the existence of any serious population 'problem' that transcends individual welfare. The aim would be to achieve the best collective decision about population issues based on knowledge of the tradeoffs between demographic choices and the 'quality of life,' however defined. This position ultimately seeks to optimize the individual and the collective decisions and then accepts the aggregate outcome—with the understanding that the situation will be reconsidered from time to time.

The second view does not deny the need for education and knowledge, but stresses the crucial gaps between what we claim as national values and the reality experienced by certain groups in our society. Many of the traditional American values, such as freedom and justice, are not yet experienced by some minorities. Racial discrimination continues to mean that equal access to opportunities afforded those in the mainstream of American society is denied to millions of people. Overt and subtle discrimination against women has meant undue pressure toward childbearing and child-rearing. Equality is denied when inadequate income, education, or racial and sexual stereotypes persist, and shape available options. Freedom is denied when governmental steps are not taken to assure the fullest possible access to methods of controlling reproduction or to educational, job, and residential opportunities. In addition, the freedom of future generations may be compromised by a denial of freedom to the present generation. Finally, extending freedom and equality—which is nothing more than making the American system live up to its stated values—would go far beyond affecting the growth rate. Full equality both for women and for racial minorities is a value in its own right. In this view, the 'population problem' is seen as only one facet, and not even a major one, of the restriction of full opportunity in American life.

The third position deals with the population problem in an

ecological framework, one whose primary axiom asserts the functional interdependence of man and his environment. It calls for a far more fundamental shift in the operative values of modern society. The need for more education and knowledge and the need to eliminate poverty and racism are important, but not enough. For the population problem, and the growth ethic with which it is intimately connected, reflect deeper external conditions and more fundamental political, economic, and philosophical values. Consequently, to improve the quality of our existence while slowing growth, will require nothing less than a basic recasting of American values.

The numbers of people and the material conditions of human existence are limited by the external environment. Human life, like all forms of life on earth, is supported by intricate ecological systems that are limited in their ability to adapt to and tolerate changing conditions. Human culture, particularly science and technology, has given man an extraordinary power to alter and manipulate his environment. At the same time, he has also achieved the capacity virtually to destroy life on earth. Sadly, in the rush to produce, consume, and discard, he has too often chosen to plunder and destroy rather than to conserve and create. Not only have the land, air, and water, the flora and fauna suffered, but also the individual, the family, and the human community.

This position holds that the present pattern of urban industrial organization, far from promoting the realization of the individual as a uniquely valuable experience, serves primarily to perpetuate its own values. Mass urban industrialism is based on science and technology, efficiency, acquisition, and domination through rationality. The exercise of these same values now contains the potential for the destruction of our humanity. Man is losing that balance with nature which is an essential condition of human existence. With that loss has come a loss of harmony with other human beings. The population problem is a concrete symptom of this change, and a fundamental cause of present human conditions.

It is comfortable to believe that changes in values or in the political system are unnecessary, and that measures such as population education and better fertility control information and services will solve our population problem. They will not, however, for such solutions do not go to the heart of man's relationship with nature, himself, and society. According to this view, nothing less than a different set of values toward nature, the transcendence of a laissez-faire market system, a redefinition of human identity in terms other than consumerism, and a radical change if not abandonment of the growth ethic, will suffice. A new vision is needed—a vision that recognizes man's unity with nature, that transcends a simple economic definition of man's identity, and that seeks to promote the realization of the highest potential of our individual humanity.

The immediate goal

These three views reflect different evaluations of the nature of the population problem, different assessments of the viability of the American political process, and different perceptions of the critical values at stake.

Given the diversity of goals to be addressed and the manifold ramifications of population change throughout society, how are specific population policies to be selected?

As a Commission and as a people, we need not agree on all the priorities if we can identify acceptable policies that speak in greater or lesser degree to all of them. By and large, in our judgment, the policy findings and recommendations of this Report meet that requirement. Whatever the primary needs of our society, the policies recommended here all lead in right directions for this nation, and generally at low costs.

Our immediate goal is to modernize demographic behaviour in this country: to encourage the American people to make population choices, both in the individual family and society at large, on the basis of greater rationality rather than tradition or custom, ignorance or chance. This country has already moved some distance down this road; it should now complete the journey. The time has come to challenge the tradition that population growth is desirable: What was unintended may turn out to be unwanted, in the society as in the family.

In any case, more rational attitudes are now forced upon us by the revolutionary increase in average length of life within the past century, which has placed modern man in a completely different, historically unique, demographic situation. The social institutions and customs that have shaped reproductive behavior in the past are no longer appropriate in the modern world, and need reshaping to suit the new situation. Moreover, the instruments of population policy are now more readily available—fuller knowledge of demographic impacts, better information on demographic trends, improved means by which individuals may control their own fertility.

As a Commission, we have come to appreciate the delicate complexities of the subject and the difficulty, even the impossibility, of solving the problem, however defined, in its entirety and all at once. But this is certainly the time to begin: The 1970s may not be simply another decade in the demographic transition but a critical one, involving changes in family life and the role of women, dynamics of the metropolitan process, the depopulation of rural areas, the movement and the needs of disadvantaged minorities, the era of the young adults produced by the baby boom, and the attendant question of what their own fertility will be—baby boom or baby bust.

Finally, we agree that population policy goals must be sought in full consonance with the fundamental values of American life: respect for human freedom, human dignity, and individual fulfillment; and concern for social justice and social welfare. To 'solve' population problems at the cost of such values would be a Pyrrhic victory indeed. The issues are ethical in character, and their proper solution requires a deep sense of moral responsibility on the part of both the individual family and the national community: the former in considering another birth, the latter in considering appropriate policies to guide population growth into the American future.

For our part, it is enough to make population, and all that it means, explicit on the national agenda, to signal its impact on our national life, to sort out the issues, and to propose how to start toward a better state of affairs. By its very nature, population is a continuing concern and should receive continuing attention. Later generations, and later commissions, will be able to see the right path further into the future. In any case, no generation needs to know the ultimate goal or the final means, only the direction in which they will be found.

SOURCE: Commission on Population Growth and the American Future, *Perspective on Population*

ROMANIA

One particularly fascinating experience in a developed country is that of Romania with abortion legislation. This extract is from a paper on the subject.

19 Drs Henry P. David and Nichols H. Wright
ABORTION IN ROMANIA

Following the lead of the Soviet Union, Romania legalized abortion on request on 25 September 1957 by Decree Number 463. The objectives were to give women the right to decide whether and when to have children, and to discourage non-qualified performers of abortions by making induced abortion by qualified practitioners more easily available (Mehlan, 1965). The right to abortion was severely restricted nine years later, on 1 October 1966. At the same time, other legal measures with pronatalist intent were introduced. It is the purpose of this paper to summarize what is known about Romanian experience before and after the changes in abortion legislation and to speculate on these findings and on the utility of legislation in attempts to influence human fertility behavior.

Historical background

In 1930 when Romania was a primarily agricultural country the birth rate was 34·1 per 1,000 population. By 1938 the birth rate had fallen to 29·5 per 1,000 population, and by 1956 it had fallen to 24·2. The decline in the Romanian birth rate appears to be associated with post-World War II industrialization and urbanization, combined with an increase in the longstanding traditional recourse to illegal abortion as a major method of limiting family size (David, 1970).

Official approval in 1957 of induced abortion on request sharply reduced illegal practices and made abortion legally, as well as socially, acceptable. Abortion centers were organized in large and medium sized hospitals, and outpatient facilities were attached to industrial plants having a sizable female work force. Women could request terminations of unwanted pregnancies within the first three months of gestation without needing prior approval of an abortion commission. Unlike the regulations in other socialist countries in central and eastern Europe, no extensive bureaucratic formalities of any kind were necessary. While name, age, number of previous births and abortions, and occupation were recorded in a register, they were not checked for veracity. Secrecy of abortion was assured.

After it had been medically determined that the unwanted pregnancy was of less than 12 weeks' duration, the abortion was usually performed immediately or within a week. Many abortions were accomplished on an outpatient basis with the woman remaining in the recovery room for about two hours. The fee was usually less than US $3.00, of which the physician received about half. Doctors worked in shifts and were permitted to perform up to ten abortions per day. Pregnancies of more than three months' duration could be terminated only in hospitals and only after medical approval had been received (Mehlan, 1965).

Liberal abortion laws

Official abortion statistics are generally not available from Romania. Mehlan (1965) learned that 112,000 abortions were performed in 1958, the first full year after induced abortion was legalized. The number of pregnancy terminations rose to 219,000 or nearly double in 1959. Relative to live births, the ratio was about 29 induced abortions per 100 live births in 1958 and 60 abortions per 100 live births in 1959. These abortion rates placed Romania immediately after Hungary in the socialist countries of central and eastern Europe. The Hungarian rate was 92 abortions per 100 live births in 1958 and 101 in 1959.

Although not representative for the country as a whole, partial reports from Bucharest and other large Romanian cities suggest that initial and repeated abortion-seeking behavior increased considerably in certain geographic areas during 1960–1962. For example, at Filantropia, the largest gynecological hospital in Bucharest, the ratio of abortions to births rose from 0·6 abortions to one birth in 1956 to 8:1 in 1959, and to 14:1 through July 1962 (Gheorghiu et al., 1963). Only 1·0 percent of induced abortions were terminated for primarily medical reasons. This suggests that a very significant percentage of abortions reflected unwanted pregnancies, interrupted for socioeconomic or other personal reasons. Summarizing Romanian studies published during 1963, Mehlan (1965) observed that 70–75 percent of women having legal abortions were in the 21–30 year age group. Approximately 8–10 percent were 20 years old or younger. About 94 percent were married. More than 50 percent of the women had had four or more previous induced abortions. Women applying for an abortion in Bucharest had had an average of 3·9 prior abortions each.

A few fragmentary abortion statistics became available after 1959. In 1966 a report was presented to the Plenum of the Romanian Communist Party Central Committee by the Ministry of Health, stating that 'the number of abortions continued to rise, reaching the figure of 1,115,000 in 1965, or four abortions for each live birth' (Romanian Ministry of Health, 1968). Based on this report the ratio of 400 abortions per 100 live births was substantially higher than the 136 abortions per 100 live births reported from Hungary. It is not clear whether total abortions for 1965 include spontaneous abortions, but it seems likely. In 1967 there were 52,083 induced (including 424 criminal) abortions and 153,700 spontaneous abortions, for a total of 205,783 (World Health Organization). The comment from Romanian sources that in 1967 there had been 'a more than five-fold drop' from the 1965 abortion peak supports the assumption that spontaneous abortions were included in the 1965 total

Monthly Birth Rates, Romania: 1966–1971

Month	1966	1967	1968	1969	1970	1971*
January	12·7	15·4	29·5	25·3	20·1	18·7
February	14·8	15·7	29·5	24·9	21·5	20·5
March	15·1	16·5	29·8	25·1	22·6	21·5
April	15·4	17·8	28·1	24·7	23·5	
May	15·2	20·7	26·8	24·1	22·3	
June	14·8	29·9	26·2	22·7	22·3	
July	14·3	38·7	26·0	23·6	22·1	
August	14·4	38·5	26·1	23·3	20·6	
September	14·1	39·9	27·8	24·9	20·8	
October	14·5†	36·1	26·4	23·0	20·5	
November	13·9	31·1	24·2	20·8	18·8	
December	12·8	27·7	21·5	17·9	18·4	
Total by year	14·3	27·3	26·8	23·3	21·1	

* Figures for 1971 are preliminary.
† Abortion policy reversed in October 1966.

SOURCES: Data for 1966–70 from Anuarul Statistic al Republicii Socialiste România, editat de Directia Centrala de Statistica and Buletin Statistic Trimestrial. Preliminary data for 1971 supplied by the Statistical Office, United Nations

(Romanian Ministry of Health, 1968). In the absence of official statistics it is difficult to evaluate the astonishing 1965 abortion figure reported by *Munca* which tends to suggest a near total dependence on abortion as a method of birth planning, at least in 1965.

During the decade of experience with liberal abortion legislation, the Romanian birth rate continued to decline, from 24·2 per 1,000 population in 1956, the year before the abortion law was liberalized, to 14·3 in 1966. It was evident that abortion had become widely available in a manner of preserving the privacy of the woman terminating an unwanted pregnancy, and that it was a socially acceptable method of birth planning. Although posters with instructions about contraception were widely displayed in abortion centers, and physicians were technically required to offer instructions in the use of contraceptive methods or to suggest insertion of an IUD after performing an abortion, there is considerable doubt about how much instruction actually occurred. It appears that modern contraception was not widely practised and did not assume a significant role in Romanian fertility behavior (David, 1970).

The legislation of October 1966

The very liberal abortion policy was abruptly reversed on 1 October 1966. The Romanian Council of State issued a decree strictly limiting the availability of abortion on request to (a) women over 45 years of age; (b) women already supporting four or more children; or (c) women whose life, in the judgment of a special commission, was endangered by the pregnancy, or who were faced with the risk of congenital deformity, or whose pregnancy resulted from rape, or who were 'physically, psychologically, or emotionally incapacitated' (Romania, 1967). More than 100 medical indications are narrowly defined in the legislation with the only leeway remaining in the psychiatric area. Although the 1966 Romanian legislation is comparatively restrictive for eastern European circumstances, it is still more liberal than that prevailing in many western European countries and North American states.

The Preamble to the October 1966 Decree refers to the 'great prejudice to the birth rate and rate of natural increase' resulting from the practice of abortion as well as to 'severe consequences to the health of women.' As Tietze (1969) comments, 'In the absence of any reports from Romania on mortality or morbidity associated with legal abortion in that country, one may conclude that the primary reason for repeal of the law of 1957 was a concern over the decline in the birth rate.' By 1963, the Romanian net reproduction rate had fallen to 0·91, indicating that the population was not replacing itself (U.N. Demographic Yearbook, 1969). In an article published in *Scientia*, Bulgaru (1966) expressed concern over the long-term effects of abortion as well as the potential dangers of laxity in abortion procedures amidst the steeply rising demand for such services.

Concomitant with the reversed abortion policy, several pronatalist measures were introduced. Family allowances were liberalized and increased (Social Security, 1969). The income tax was reduced 30 percent for families with three or more children (Sadvokasova, 1969). The 'childlessness' tax was reintroduced and levied on men and women over 26 years of age, whether single or married. The basis on which the government paid a birth allowance also changed in late 1966. Formerly, a birth allowance equivalent to about $85.00 was paid to the parents of all tenth and later births on the basis of the birth certificate. Parents having a third or later birth became eligible for this lump sum payment beginning 1 January 1967 (Romania, 1966).

Romania: Divorce Rates per 1,000 Population

Year	Rate
1965	1·94
1966	1·35
1967	<0·01
1968	0·20
1969	0·35 (Provisional)

SOURCE: UN, *Demographic Yearbook* (1969)

Official importation of contraceptives ceased, but their sale was not prohibited. Divorces for couples with children under 16 years of age were made more difficult to obtain. The divorce process was lengthened, requiring a trial period of reconciliation of six months for families without children and one year for those with children. This explains why the number of divorces fell from about 25,000 in 1966 to 48 in 1967. As shown in the table on p 125, the divorce rate increased in 1968, and again in 1969, but remained less than 20 percent of the 1965 rate.

Effects of restrictive legislation
The dramatic effect of the October 1966 legislation is apparent in the table on p 123 and below. After promulgation of the

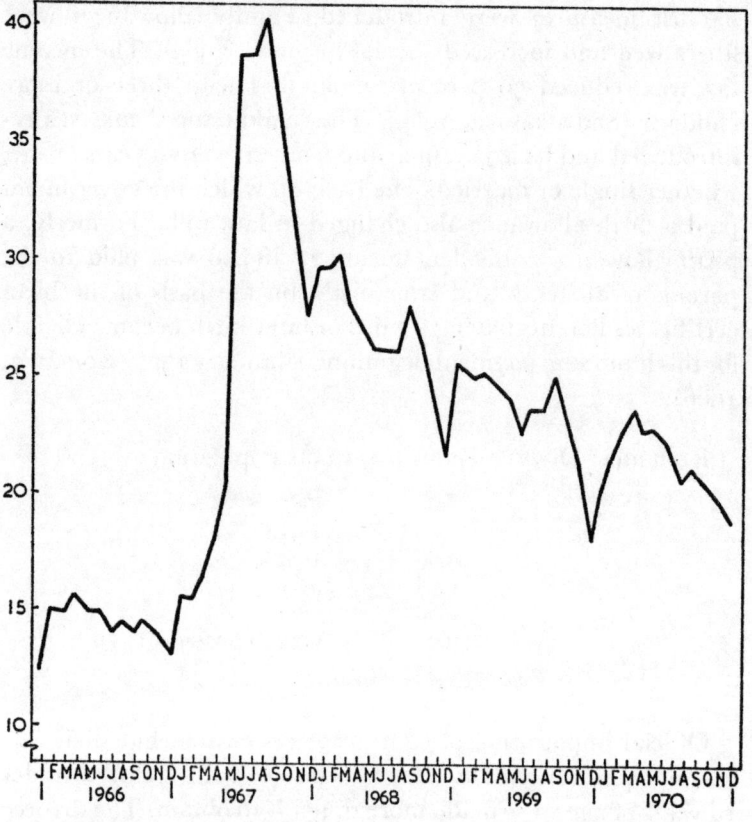

Monthly birth rates per 1,000 population, Romania, 1966–70

decree, the birth rate rose from a low of 12·8 per 1,000 population in December 1966 to 39·9 in September 1967. Since December 1966, the birth rate has gradually decreased, almost steadily on a month-by-month basis, as also shown in the table. Initial effects of the legislation were reported and discussed by Ferenbac (1969) at the London Congress of the International Union for the Scientific Study of Population. Annual birth rates per 1,000 population rose from the low of 14·3 in 1966 to 27·3 in 1967 but subsequently declined again to 26·8 in 1968, 23·3 in 1969, and 21·1 in 1970. A further fall in 1971 appears likely, but the rate of decline has decreased since 1968.

What conclusions can be drawn from the gradual decline of the Romanian birth rate after its initial upward spurt following the sudden reimposition of legal restrictions on induced abortion? Perhaps the most pragmatic reason for the increase in the monthly birth rate from the low of 12·8 per 1,000 population in December 1966 to the high of 39·9 in September 1967 is that Romanian couples required time and experience to adjust to the constraints of a decree which suddenly and severely restricted access to previously easily available legal abortion. This conclusion receives some support from Ferenbac's (1971) observation that the differential between urban and rural birth rates became minimal in 1967, but that the previous divergence reappeared in 1968 and became stronger in 1969. Although the birth rate continues to decline, it is too early to predict with certainty where or when a levelling off will occur. It is also true that in late 1966, the number of Romanian women at risk of live birth was at a maximum. As these women remained pregnant and carried their pregnancies to term, the proportion of fecundable women declined which, in turn, led to birth rate decline.

One hypothesis for explaining the reported declines in the birth rate is that the traditional Romanian preference for a small family was not seriously affected by the shift in legislation. In the absence of a fundamental change in motivation for limiting family size and engaging in family planning, it seems unlikely that legal restrictions on abortion, coupled with more benevolent pronatalist welfare provisions, will result in more than a short-term increase in the birth rate, a rise that apparently has been associated with increased mortality, and probably morbidity of mothers and children. The Romanian experience suggests that well-established behavioral patterns of fertility control are resistant to significantly prolonged change by governmental edict alone.

SOURCE: Population Council, *Studies in Family Planning* (October 1971)

Romania, incidentally, was the venue for the 21st Pugwash Conference on Science and World Affairs in August 1971. The scientists attending adopted a statement which said:

20 Pugwash and Environmental Future Conferences STATEMENTS, 1971

Although the rate of population growth differs widely among countries the rapid increase in world population is an alarming threat to the future of mankind. In many less developed countries the annual increase in population is virtually as large as the annual increase in production. Also the increase in population in the highly developed countries is serious. In many technologically developed countries the depletion of natural resources and pollution will cause eventually serious consequences if the countries delay too long to take steps to limit the increase in population.

A conference earlier in the year, the International Conference on Environmental Future, which met at Jyvaskyla, Finland, from 27 June to 3 July 1971, issued the following statement.

Man is also the victim of the excessive mutiplication of his own species: unbridled population increases are causing social, political and environmental problems over an increasingly large part of the world and defeating the legitimate aspirations of mankind. Therefore, the need for population control is urgent in most parts of the world. Since developed countries consume a large portion of the world's resources, population control is necessary in nearly all of them in order to reduce pressure on natural resources throughout the world. Equally population control is necessary in most of the less developed lands where population pressures impede economic advance. It is unlikely that enough food can be produced and distributed to sustain the world population in the next thirty years after which time the present number will have doubled, unless vigorous programmes of population control are systematically pursued.

PART FOUR

Obstacles to Action

THE ROMAN CATHOLIC CHURCH

On 29 July 1968 Pope Paul issued the now famous encyclical Humanae Vitae. *Probably no other event was of greater importance for the population and family planning movement during the 1960s. Here are extracts from the Encyclical itself.*

21A Papal Encyclical
HUMANAE VITAE

The transmission of life

1. The most serious duty of transmitting human life, for which married persons are the free and responsible collaborators of God the Creator, has always been a source of great joys for them, even if sometimes accompanied by not a few difficulties and by distress.

At all times the fulfilment of this duty has posed grave problems to the conscience of married persons, but, with the recent evolution of society, changes have taken place that give rise to new questions which the Church could not ignore, having to do with a matter which so closely touches upon the life and happiness of men.

I New aspects of the problem and competency of the Magisterium

New formulation of the problem

2. The changes which have taken place are in fact noteworthy and of varied kinds. In the first place, there is the rapid demographic development. Fear is shown by many that world population is growing more rapidly than the available resources, with growing distress to many families and developing countries, so that the temptation for authorities to counter this danger with radical measures is great. Moreover, working and lodging conditions, as well as increased exigencies both in the economic field and in that of education, often make the proper education of an elevated number of children difficult today.

A change is also seen both in the manner of considering the person of woman and her place in society, and in the value to be attributed to conjugal love in marriage, and also in the appreciation to be made of the meaning of conjugal acts in relation to that love.

Finally and above all, man has made stupendous progress in the domination and rational organization of the forces of nature, such that he tends to extend this domination to his own total being; to the body, to physical life, to social life and even to the laws which regulate the transmission of life.

3. This new state of things gives rise to new questions. Granted the conditions of life today, and granted the meaning which conjugal relations have with respect to the harmony between husband and wife and to their mutual fidelity, would not a revision of the ethical norms in force up to now seem to be advisable, especially when it is considered that they cannot be observed without sacrifices, sometimes heroic sacrifices?

And again: by extending to this field the application of the so-called 'principle of totality' could it not be admitted that the intention of a less abundant but more rationalized fecundity might transform a materially sterilizing intervention into a licit and wise control of birth?

Could it not be admitted, that is, that the finality of procreation pertains to the ensemble of conjugal life, rather than to its single acts? It is also asked whether, in view of the increased sense of responsibility of modern man, the moment has not come for him to entrust to his reason and his will, rather than to the biological rhythms of his organism, the task of regulating birth.

Competency of the Magisterium
4. Such questions required from the teaching authority of the Church a new and deeper reflection upon the principles of the moral teaching on marriage: a teaching founded on the natural law, illuminated and enriched by divine Revelation.

No believer will wish to deny that the teaching authority of the Church is competent to interpret even the natural moral law. It is, in fact, indisputable, as our predecessors have many times declared, that Jesus Christ, when communicating to Peter and to the Apostles His divine authority and sending them to teach all nations His commandments, constituted them as guardians and authentic interpreters of all the moral law, not only, that is, of the law of the gospel, but also of the natural law, which is also an expression of the will of God, the faithful fulfilment of which is equally necessary for salvation.

Comformably to this mission of hers, the Church has always provided—and even more amply in recent times—a coherent teaching concerning both the nature of marriage and the correct use of conjugal rights and the duties of husband and wife.

Special studies
5. The consciousness of that same mission induced us to confirm and enlarge the study commission which our predecessor Pope John XXIII of happy memory had instituted in March, 1963. That commission which included besides several experts in the various pertinent disciplines, also married couples, had as its scope the gathering of opinions on the new questions regarding conjugal life, and in particular on the regulation of births, and of furnishing opportune elements of information so

that the magisterium could give an adequate reply to the expectation not only of the faithful but also of world opinion.

The work of these experts, as well as the successive judgments and counsels spontaneously forwarded by or expressly requested from a good number of our brothers in the episcopate, have permitted us to measure more exactly all the aspects of this complex matter. Hence with all our heart we express to each of them, our lively gratitude.

Reply to the Magisterium
6. The conclusions at which the commission arrived could not, nevertheless, be considered by us as definitive, nor dispense us from a personal examination of this serious question; and this also because, within the commission itself, no full concordance of judgments concerning the moral norms to be proposed had been reached, and above all because certain criteria of solutions had emerged which departed from the moral teaching on marriage proposed with constant firmness by the teaching authority of the Church.

Therefore, having attentively sifted the documentation laid before us, after mature reflexion and assiduous prayers, we now intend, by virtue of the mandate entrusted to us by Christ, to give our reply to these grave questions.

II Doctrinal principles

A total vision of man
7. The problem of birth, like every other problem regarding human life, is to be considered beyond partial perspectives whether of the biological or psychological, demographic or sociological orders—in the light of an integral vision of man and of his vocation, not only his natural and earthly, but also his supernatural and eternal vocation. And since, in the attempt to justify artificial methods of birth control, many have appealed to the demands both of conjugal love and of 'responsible parenthood', it is good to state very precisely the true

concept of these two great realities of married life, referring principally to what was recently set forth in this regard, and in a highly authoritative form, by the Second Vatican Council in its Pastoral Constitution 'Gaudium et Spes'.

Conjugal love
8. Conjugal love reveals its true nature and nobility when it is considered in its supreme origin, God, Who is Love, 'the Father, from whom every family in heaven and on earth is named.'

Marriage is not, then, the effect of chance or the product of evolution of unconscious natural forces; it is the wise institution of the Creator to realize in mankind His design of love. By means of the reciprocal personal gift of self, proper and exclusive to them, husband and wife tend towards the communion of their beings in view of mutual personal perfection, to collaborate with God in the generation and education of new lives.

For baptized persons, moreover, marriage invests the dignity of a sacramental sign of grace, inasmuch as it represents the union of Christ and of the Church.

Its characteristics
9. Under this light, there clearly appear the characteristic marks and demands of conjugal love, and it is of supreme importance to have an exact idea of these.

This love is first of all fully human, that is to say, of the senses and of the spirit at the same time. It is not, then, a simple transport of instinct and sentiment, but also, and principally, an act of the free will intended to endure and to grow by means of the joys and sorrows of daily life, in such a way that husband and wife become one only heart and one only soul, and together attain their human perfection.

Then, this love is total, that is to say, it is a very special form of personal friendship, in which husband and wife generously share everything, without undue reservations or selfish calcula-

tions. Whoever truly loves his marriage partner loves not only for what he receives, but for the partner's self, rejoicing that he can enrich his partner with the gift of himself.

Again, this love is faithful and exclusive until death. Thus, in fact, do bride and groom conceive it to be on the day when they freely and in full awareness assume the duty of the marriage bond. A fidelity, this, which can sometimes be difficult, but is always possible, always noble and meritorious, as no one can deny. The example of so many married persons down through the centuries shows, not only that fidelity is according to the nature of marriage, but also that it is a source of profound and lasting happiness.

And finally, this love is fecund, for it is not exhausted by the communion between husband and wife, but is destined to continue, raising up new lives. 'Marriage and conjugal love are by their nature ordained toward the begetting and educating of children. Children are really the supreme gift of marriage and contribute very substantially to the welfare of their parents.'

Responsible parenthood

10. Hence conjugal love requires in husband and wife an awareness of their mission of 'responsible parenthood,' which today is rightly much insisted upon, and which also must be exactly understood. Consequently it is to be considered under different aspects which are legitimate and connected with one another.

In relation to the biological processes, responsible parenthood means the knowledge and respect of their functions; human intellect discovers in the power of giving life biological laws which are part of the human person.

In relation to the tendencies of instinct or passion, responsible parenthood means that necessary dominion which reason and will must exercise over them.

In relation to physical, economic, psychological and social conditions, responsible parenthood is exercised, either by the deliberate and generous decision to raise a numerous family or by the decision, made for grave motives and with due respect for the moral law, to avoid for the time being, or even for an indeterminate period a new birth.

Responsible parenthood also and above all implies a more profound relationship to the objective moral order established by God, of which a right conscience is the faithful interpreter. The responsible exercise of parenthood implies, therefore, that husband and wife recognise fully their own duties towards God, towards themselves, towards the family and towards society, as a correct hierarchy of values.

In the task of transmitting life, they are not free to proceed completely at will, as if they could determine in a wholly autonomous way the honest path to follow; but they must conform their activity to the creative intention of God, expressed in the very nature of marriage and of its acts, and manifested by the constant teaching of the Church.

Respect for the nature and purposes of the marriage act
11. These acts, by which husband and wife are united in chaste intimacy, and by means of which human life is transmitted, are, as the Council recalled, 'noble and worthy,' and they do not cease to be lawful if, for causes independent of the will of husband and wife, they are foreseen to be infecund, since they always remain ordained towards expressing and consolidating their union.

In fact, as experience bears witness, not every conjugal act is followed by a new life. God has wisely disposed natural laws and rhythms of fecundity which, of themselves, cause a separation in the succession of births. Nonetheless, the Church, calling men back to the observance of the norms of the natural law, as interpreted by her constant doctrine, teaches that each and every marriage act ('quilibet matrimonii usus') must remain open to the transmission of life.

Two inseparable aspects: union and procreation
12. That teaching, often set forth by the magisterium, is

founded upon the inseparable connexion, willed by God and unable to be broken by man on his own initiative, between the two meanings of the conjugal act; the unitive meaning and the procreative meaning. Indeed, by its intimate structure, the conjugal act, while most closely uniting husband and wife, capacitates them for the generation of new lives, according to laws inscribed in the very being of man and of woman.

By safeguarding both these essential aspects, the unitive and the procreative, the conjugal act preserves in its fulness the sense of true mutual love and its ordination towards man's most high calling to parenthood. We believe that the men of our day are particularly capable of seizing the deeply reasonable and human character of this fundamental principle.

Faithfulness to God's design
13. It is in fact justly observed that a conjugal act imposed upon one's partner without regard for his or her condition and lawful desires is not a true act of love, and therefore denies an exigency of right moral order in the relationships between husband and wife. Hence, one who reflects well must also recognize that a reciprocal act of love, which jeopardizes the disponibility to transmit life which God the Creator, according to particular laws, inserted therein, is in contradiction with the design constitutive of marriage, and with the will of the Author of life.

To use this divine gift destroying, even if only partially, its meaning and its purpose is to contradict the nature both of man and of woman and of their most intimate relationship, and therefore it is to contradict also the plan of God and His will. On the other hand, to make use of the gift of conjugal love while respecting the laws of the generative process means to acknowledge oneself not to be the arbiter of the sources of human life, but rather the minister of the design established by the Creator.

In fact, just as man does not have unlimited dominion over his body in general, so also, with particular reason, he has no such dominion over his generative faculties as such, because of their intrinsic ordination towards raising up life, of which God is the principle. 'Human life is sacred', Pope John XXIII recalled, 'from its very inception it reveals the creating hand of God.'

Illicit ways of regulating birth
14. In conformity with these landmarks in the human and Christian vision of marriage, we must once again declare that the direct interruption of the generative process already begun, and, above all, directly willed and procured abortion, even if for therapeutic reasons, are to be absolutely excluded as licit means of regulating birth.

Equally to be excluded, as the teaching authority of the Church has frequently declared, is direct sterilization, whether perpetual or temporary, whether of the man or of the woman. Similarly excluded is every action which, either in anticipation of the conjugal act, or in its accomplishment, or in the development of its natural consequences, proposes, whether as an end or as a means, to render procreation impossible.

To justify conjugal acts made intentionally infecund, one cannot invoke as valid reasons the lesser evil, or the fact that such acts would constitute a whole together with the fecund acts already performed or to follow later, and hence would share in one and the same moral goodness.

In truth, if it is sometimes licit to tolerate a lesser evil in order to avoid a greater evil or to promote a greater good, it is not licit, even for the gravest reasons, to do evil so that good may follow therefrom, that is, to make into the object of a positive act of the will something which is intrinsically disorder, and hence unworthy of the human person, even when the intention is to safeguard or promote individual, family or social well-being. Consequently it is an error to think that a conjugal act which is deliberately made infecund be made honest and right by the ensemble of a fecund conjugal life.

Licitness of therapeutic means
15. The Church, on the contrary, does not at all consider illicit the use of those therapeutic means truly necessary to cure diseases of the organism, even if an impediment to procreation, which may be foreseen, should result therefrom, provided such impediment is not, for whatever motive, directly willed.

Licitness of recourse to informed periods
16. To this teaching of the Church on conjugal morals, the objection is made today, as we observed earlier, that it is the prerogative of the human intellect to dominate the energies offered by irrational nature and to orientate them towards an end conformable to the good of man.

Now, some may ask: In the present case, is it not reasonable in many circumstances to have recourse to artificial birth control if, thereby, we secure the harmony and peace of the family, and better conditions for the education of the children already born? To this question it is necessary to reply with clarity: The Church is the first to praise and recommend the intervention of intelligence in a function which so closely associates the rational creature with his Creator; but she affirms that this must be done with respect for the order established by God.

If, then, there are serious motives to space out births, which derive from the physical or psychological conditions of husband and wife, or from external conditions, the Church teaches that it is then licit to take into account the natural rhythms immanent in the generative functions, for the use of marriage in the infecund periods only, and in this way to regulate birth without offending the moral principles which have been recalled earlier.

SOURCE: *The Times* (1 August 1968)

The following reaction to the Encyclical was prepared by Dr Leo

Alting Von Geusau, a Dutch Catholic priest, and founder and secretary-general of the Interdenominational Centre for International Documentation on the Contemporary Church.

21B Dr Leo Alting Von Geusau
INTERNATIONAL REACTION TO THE ENCYCLICAL 'HUMANAE VITAE'

There has probably been no other document of the head of the Roman Catholic Church that has provoked so many and such contradictory reactions, not only inside the Roman Catholic Church and in all christian churches, but in non-christian churches and secular institutions as well. In the Roman Catholic Church, *Humanae Vitae* caused the greatest movement of dissent since the Reformation. It is possible that in some cases the Encyclical simply made visible tensions already existing—tensions between conservatives and liberals, between theologians and the Church hierarchy, and between bishops and the papacy. Outside the Roman Catholic Church, the reactions were also strong. By directing *Humanae Vitae* to 'all men of good will' and by appealing to the 'natural law,' Pope Paul VI had addressed himself to the personal and, in some cases, professional lives of all men.

The following material on reactions to *Humanae Vitae* was obtained from documents collected at the Center for International Documentation on the Contemporary Church (IDO-C), an independent, interdenominational, and international agency, with headquarters in Rome. Between August 1968 and May 1969, the center received about 4000 reactions, in the form of newspaper articles, magazine articles, pamphlets, and books.

This report will interpret the reaction from three perspectives: (1) a geographical point of view, distinguishing mainly the political and the religious (or ideological) aspects; (2) a specialist point of view, distinguishing demographers, economists, local practitioners, psychologists, psychiatrists, obstetricians, biologists, theologians, and philosophers; and (3) an ecumenical point of view, noting the effect of the Encyclical on the relationships between different religions.

Geographical approach

Governments and political leaders
The Philippine Government reacted immediately to *Humanae Vitae*. A few days after the proclamation of the Encyclical, the Government cancelled its recently approved family planning project. This was on the request of Cardinal Santos, the head of the Philippine Roman Catholic hierarchy.

In Colombia, which has a Concordat with the Vatican, the minister of Foreign Affairs, German Zea Hernandez, was asked to resign after he had openly criticized the papal statement as interference in the political processes of the country.

In Japan, the Roman Catholic hierarchy has not yet issued a Japanese translation of the Encyclical, thus avoiding open conflict with the Government.

The situation in India was ambiguous, with both the Government and the Catholic hierarchy remaining silent. Cardinal Gracias, the leading member of the Indian hierarchy, has been somewhat sympathetic to family planning efforts; at the same time he has been concerned with maintaining a good relationship with Rome. When *Humanae Vitae* was issued, Cardinal Gracias expressed support for it, but he did not attempt to suppress dissent: a nationwide seminar in Bangalore in March 1969, composed of priests and laymen from the whole of India, asked the Vatican for further development of the doctrine on marriage. The collective hierarchy of India later issued a statement favorable to *Humanae Vitae*.

Spain and Portugal, both of which have Concordats with the Vatican, clearly supported the Pope. They were, strangely enough, in the company of some small Communist governments, like Cuba and Albania. These two Communist countries applauded the Vatican for taking a stand against what they considered the corruption of western bourgeois imperialists and their oppressive family planning efforts.

Many Latin American governments did not express their views directly and immediately; their reactions, in general, were favorable to the Encyclical. In general, their support had a political, rather than a theological or moral basis. It had been evident since the press conference of Robert McNamara, President of the International Bank for Reconstruction and Development, in October 1968 in Buenos Aires for the Society of Inter-American Press, where he emphasized the necessity of slowing rapid population growth, that Latin American public opinion has been sensitive on this subject. Bishop Helder Camara of Recife expressed this view on September 28, 1968:

> 'The Latin American, Asiatic and African masses, would quite quickly have been filled and overwhelmed with contraceptive pills, had not Pope Paul VI issued the encyclical *Humanae Vitae*. We shall never forget the words of President Johnson when he stated: "Five dollars spent for birth control are rather more profitable than a hundred dollars to favor development." I am therefore grateful to Pope Paul VI for his encyclical, even if I recognize that it might create problems for developing countries.'

This statement has a tone similar to the statements of Juan Bosch, ex-President of the Dominican Republic; Chilean Government officials; and the former Bolivian President Rene Barrientos. All opposed an American population policy, which since 1969 has been called 'preventive genocide' or 'basic panacea.' The review *Oiga* in Lima, in an article called 'McNamara Undertakes Escalation against Latin America,' suggested that Paul VI, foreseeing the initiative of the World Bank, had issued the Encyclical.

The Latin American position is complicated. Some governments have agreements with the United States to educate the people in the use of artificial means of birth control. At the same time, most of these same governments have close relationships with the Roman Catholic hierarchy of their country.

Before the Encyclical it was clear from a statement of Arias Stela, the Minister of Health of Peru, that his government and the Roman Catholic herarchy of the country had agreed on the use of the pill in certain cases. However, after the Encyclical, it appeared that the accent would shift to the general principle of education to responsible parenthood.

Parallels to this reaction can be found in some satellite Communist countries in Eastern Europe, vis-à-vis the Russian demographic policy, and also among minority groups in the United States.

In black Africa there was general approval of the Encyclical. This approval was not expressed in terms comparable to those of the Latin American experts cited above. Many of the African states have small populations, and for some time many political and religious leaders have emphasized the benefits of large families.

Roman Catholic hierarchy

Two distinctions should be made here: (1) between the episcopal conferences (generally the national unities of bishops) and the individual bishops; and (2) between the official and the confidential reactions of the bishops.

In general, it can be said that the Synod of Bishops, held in Rome October 12–29, 1969, had been convened by the Pope in response to the authority conflict raised between the bishops and the Pope over *Humanae Vitae*. The Synod stated that the Holy See should not issue documents or make major decisions without consulting the episcopal conferences.

A year earlier, between August and November 1968, most of the episcopal conferences reacted in an ambiguous way. In countries where many bishops, government officials, and public opinion were in favor of the Encyclical, the conferences came out with clear statements. Conferences in black Africa, the Philippines, as well as in Concordat countries such as Spain and Portugal, came out with favorable statements. Bishops behind the Iron Curtain, as well as conferences in some Asian countries such as India, Vietnam, and Korea, also announced support (although in some cases support conflicted with the government's policy).

Reactions in western countries were different. The Dutch bishops were the first to react with a statement to their priests on August 4, 1968:

> 'In the formation of the conscience an authoritative role should be given to the word of the magistery, even if in this case of *Humanae Vitae* we are not faced with an infallible teaching. The priests and the faithful have therefore to study the document carefully, giving however, the last word to the individual conscience.'

This became the pattern of reaction of the German, Belgian, Austrian, Canadian, Swiss, British, Irish, Indonesian, Australian, South African, Scandinavian, and the United States Catholic Conferences.

These reactions were phrased in different ways. The United States bishops related the question of birth control to that of conscientious objection, suggesting that in exceptional cases the individual conscience may oppose a generally accepted law. The Dutch and the Belgians almost suggested the contrary to this. In these countries emphasis is placed on the importance of individual conscience, giving individual freedom to accept or reject church teaching.

The French and Italian bishops, apart from reference to the individual conscience, spoke of the collision of two laws when they characterized as the aims of marriage: the law of love and the law of procreation.

The Latin American bishops generally approved the papal statement. However, the Chileans raised the issue of the question of conscience. In a continent-wide congress in Medellín, Colombia, in August 1968, to which Pope Paul paid a visit, they approved a document expressing concern about the population problem and emphasizing the importance of education to responsible parenthood.

To all this, it should be added that by no means did all episcopal conferences react to *Humanae Vitae*.

Individual reactions were many. Some roman curia prelates and cardinals spoke of the Pope as the saviour of mankind who had constructed a barrier against modern paganism. The French-born bishop, Cardinal Tisserant, predicted that posterity would consider Pope Paul as the great prophet. Cardinal Leger from Canada and Cardinal Journet from Switzerland expressed similar statements. In the United States, Cardinals McIntyre and O'Boyle stated that they would excommunicate anybody who would not unconditionally accept the literal teaching of the Encyclical.

Other individuals expressed great reserve toward the Encyclical. Within a year after the appearance of the Encyclical Bishop Shannon, auxiliary of St. Paul, Minnesota, left his ministry. This was also the case of Bishop Larrain, auxiliary of Santiago de Chile. Also expressing opposition were the South African white Bishops Van Velsen and Hurley. Bishop Simons of Lahore, India, issued a book on the occasion of *Humanae Vitae*, in which he expressed doubts as to the traditional and popular concept of infallibility. The Italian Cardinal Pelegrino told a press conference that papal doctrine might change in the future. Cardinal Cushing of Boston said 'Roma locuta, causa finita, if Rome has spoken, the question has been decided upon . . . at least for the moment.'

Specialists' approach

Demographers and economists
Those involved in demographic studies or programs reacted very strongly to *Humanae Vitae*; western economists and demographers more so than those from developing countries.

The September 1968 issue of the British *Economist* stated that the Pope spoiled an initial awareness in Roman Catholic developing countries of the population problem. It added: '. . . even in other developing countries, not of Catholic majority, the poor will pay for this error of the Pope.'

Some viewed the Encyclical as a danger to the future of mankind. Addeke Boerma, Dutch-born director of the United Nations Food and Agriculture Organization, said:

'The demographic expansion without population control can easily destroy the benefits modern technology brings to developing countries. . . . I cannot make a judgment on religious motivations . . . but like other organizations of the U. N., preoccupied by the rise in the cost of living in developing countries, I think that birth control has to become an intrinsic element of an essential infrastructure which is indispensable in the improvement of living conditions for mankind.'

A group of 2,600 American scientists issued the following statement:

'The scientists who have signed this document strongly protest against the encyclical of Paul VI, *Humanae Vitae*, on birth control. More than half of the globe suffers from hunger and its social conditions are deteriorating rapidly, perhaps in an irrevocable way. The menace of contagion on a world level augments. . . . Demographic pressure contributes to political tension and increases the probability of bacteriological and atomic warfare. Each action trying to prevent the efforts to stop numerical development of world population sanctions the misery in which millions of men are living today, and at the same time makes the death of a still higher number in future decades inevitable. . . . The world should be aware as quickly as possible that Paul VI has sanctioned the death of endless numbers of human beings with his wrongly inspired and immoral encylical.'

The strong language of the document caused many specialists to withdraw their signature although they agreed with the substance of the statement.

Italian scientist Adriano Buzzati Traverso, in the August 11, 1968 issue of *Expresso*, spoke of the demographic problems of a western European country like Italy, and said that the poor people from the south (Calabria and Sicily), who are in need of education for responsible parenthood, would be more inclined to accept the authority of the Church on birth control. He added:

'It is well-known that today 350 million children aged six years and under, i.e., 70 per cent of the children in that age group, show an abnormal growth rate, inferior to the average of normal well-fed children. They are apathetic, easily irritable and unresponsive to educational processes. . . . [These are the results of kwashiorkor and culebrilla, two diseases caused by lack of protein.] For the modern scientist it is as natural to use antibiotics to control mortality, as it is to control or to forestall the conception of children; a process destined to suffer the consequences of old taboos from old traditions of about three centuries ago, when it was thought that the sun revolves around the earth, even if scientific facts cast doubts on whether the earth is the center of the universe, or the See of Peter, the center of mankind. . . .'

'Bigotry, pedantry and fanaticism,' said the British *New Scientist*, 'can kill, mutilate and torment their victims just as well as bombs, pogroms and gas chambers. . . .'

A group of Puerto Rican specialists issued a strong denunciatory statement in December 1968.

Dutch Jesuit economist Louis Janssen said, on August 17, 1968, that the 'decision of the Pope will seriously delay the solution of the demographic problem.'

A group of Latin American specialists expressed concern at a congress on population problems held at the end of July 1968, sponsored by the Organization of American States (Organizacion de Estados Americanos) and its advisory committee, the Advisory Committee on Population and Development (Comité Asesor en Población y Desarrollo).

The August 7, 1968 editorial of *Accion* in Lima stated:

'The successor to Pope John [who was human and realistic] has created an option for the principle of authority, that *wants* to be spiritual, but *is* to command . . . He wants a society, composed of poor families, horrified by the fear of a new conception, a world of misery and under-nourishment. . . .'

The presidents of the Roman Catholic Family Movement in Brazil, Antonio and Margarida Acauan, stated in *Ponto Homen*, December 1968:

'How can the analphabets [those who cannot read or write] of Brazil, i.e., 50 per cent of the population, register numbers, indicate dates, make accounts, verify thermometers. . . . Thousands of poor women knock on the doors of the family planning clinics: it is after all Christ they are seeking [to help them out of their misery] and to whom they appeal. . . .'

From this last and from other examples, it is clear that some Roman Catholic specialists, in the years prior to the Encyclical, had been critical of the old adage reiterated by Paul VI: 'To multiply the bread on the table, not to diminish the eaters.' This attitude was expressed not only in the Papal Commission which studied the demographic aspects of the question of birth control from 1964–68, but also by the Beirut Conference, April 1968, sponsored by the World Council of Churches and the Papal Commission Justitia et Pax. 'Without drastic changes, we must see that a great part of the human family will continue to be undernourished and that tens of millions of children will grow up with diminished intelligence and energy.' This was the conclusion of a paper by Richard Fagley and Arthur McCormack at the Conference (censored by the Vatican).

In some cases, the concern over the Encyclical was concentrated on the problem of abortion. This was the case in Italy, where there is a very high rate of induced abortions (some statistics estimate an average of three to four abortions per woman aged 18 to 45).

Father Dexter Hanley, Director of the Center for Human Rights at Georgetown University, stated in the August 1968 bulletin of the Population Reference Bureau that the abortion rate in Latin America was increasing alarmingly, and added: 'Because abortion is socially and morally a much greater evil [than contraception], contraception programs can be justified, at least by the principle of having to accept the lesser evil.'

In the October 3, 1968 issue of the Russian *Literaturnaya Gazeta*, George Speransky commented: 'The Pope condemns millions of women to the practice of abortion. Only a wicked and cruel man could forbid effective and inoffensive methods of contraception.'

At a pharmaceutical world congress in Hamburg in September 1968, Professor Gerhardt Martius, gynaecologist from Berlin, said: 'The essential aim of birth control is to prevent the present multiplication of abortions with all its inherent dangers.'

Others, however, did not view the Encyclical as a danger for the future of mankind: they believed that *Humanae Vitae* would not particularly affect the existing contraceptive practice among Roman Catholics. This opinion was expressed in *Le Journal de l'Université et des Facultés Françaises* on November 1, 1968.

Not all of those concerned with problems of population and economic development were unsympathetic to the Papal Encyclical. Dr. Ulrich Koch, Director General of the German Roman Catholic aid program, in the September 9, 1968 issue of *Misereor*, stated: 'The Pope has clearly said that in order to resolve the demographic problem in underdeveloped countries, unjust structures of the society have to be done away with and replaced by more just ones.' Chilean professor Hubnar Gallo, in his book *The Myth of the Demographic Explosion*, asserted that there was no population problem on his continent. 'The demographic explosion is a pseudo-problem,' said the Argentinian review *7 Dias Ilustrados*, on October 2, 1968. Argentinian Julio Notta said in his book *Crisis and Solution of the Argentinian Foreign Trade*: 'From what nature offers us together with increased technical possibilities, there are at present sufficient means to feed a population five or six times higher than the actual population of the planet ... if there is a lack of food, it is because the economic organization is bad and unjust.' Roque Adames, Rector of the Roman Catholic university in Santo Domingo, said: 'The solution to the demographic problem is not to corrupt mankind in his moral foundations, but to educate him so that he may make more rational use of his resources.'

Health specialists
Two generalizations can be made about the reactions of gyne-

cologists, doctors, psychologists, psychiatrists, and biologists. On the one hand, those more involved in the day-to-day life of the family—e.g., those concerned with marital relationships and with the raising of children—tended to react negatively to the Encyclical. This category would include house doctors, psychiatrists, psychologists, and gynaecologists. On the other hand, those more involved in scientific research and, in particular, in research on the pill shared some of the Pope's concern. The medical experts on the Papal Commission had expressed reservations about the safety of the pill to the Pope, but they recommended that the Pope not take a stand on the issue and leave it to the advice of specialists.

Dutch Roman Catholic gynecologist and pediatrician C. P. Sporken, early in August 1968, opposed what he called 'the Pope's drawback on biologism.' Jan Snijders, Roman Catholic psychologist and Rector of the University of Groningen (Holland), followed him by saying: 'I cannot see the Encyclical as a religious document, as a message of Christ.' 'To limit sex relations to infertile periods, would have psychotic effects,' commented an anonymous Peruvian psychiatrist.

French hospital gynecologist Michael Chartier commented: 'The Catholic gynecologist finds himself torn between the decisions of the teaching of the Church and daily life of the couple ... one can doubt the value of a law which seems to consider all women as if they always had perfectly timed ovulation cycles, since 20 per cent of them are exceptions to the general norm.'

'Paul VI is completely unrealistic and in conflict with the discoveries of modern science,' stated the German Catholic Medical Guild on October 1, 1968. R. Géraud, a French maternity psychologist, added: 'Human intervention scientifically studied and sufficiently secure, cannot negatively influence the person.' 'Almost all commentaries on the Encyclical are in favor of temporary sterilization of the woman by chemical means,' concluded Pierre Grasset from Paris. The Italian Association of Catholic Doctors agreed: 'The Encyclical contains incomprehensible contradictions ... from a medical point of view.' This belief was expressed by the General Assembly of the National Center of Catholic Doctors, an Algerian team of doctors, and the World Federation of Mental Health which met in August 1968.

Very few physicians took the occasion of *Humanae Vitae* to reassert claims that periodic abstinence can be a highly effective means of family planning.

The reactions of researchers took a different perspective. Dr. Emil Ottuli and Robert Nickolson from Buenos Aires viewed the Encyclical as an opportunity to re-examine the question of the pill. 'I am against the pill, not because of moral or religious prejudices, but after serious reflections on its consequences,' said the French sexologist Paul Chauchard.

Luigi Gedda, Italian specialist in pregnancy and twins, said that it was the Pope's task to warn everyone about the risks of taking the pill. The commentary of the Russian Verbenko seemed to suggest the skepticism of some Russian doctors about the pill.

Most researchers, while sharing the concern over the existing forms of chemical contraceptives, were critical of the Pope's declaration over a technical field; some feared that the Encyclical would hamper the development of better methods of contraception. Only a few believed that improved methods were impossible.

James Mastboom, Dutch gynecologist and a researcher on the pill, expressed his concern over existing chemical contraceptives on August 1, 1968; but he believed that the actual margin of uncertainty in periodic abstinence could be reduced to 5 per cent and that improved therapeutic methods could be developed.

Whether or not the Encyclical will stimulate research on contraceptives cannot be determined. An American obstetrician said: 'No one has stimulated more the research for new contraceptives than the last three popes, because of their strong stand against existing methods; is not Dr. Rock a Roman

Catholic?' A well-financed research center for the study of new methods of family planning was opened in Paris soon after the proclamation of the Encyclical.

Theologians and philosophers
Humanae Vitae touched upon a great number of topics in theology, and, to some extent, philosophy. Reactions from theologians were immediate and world-wide.

The question of papal authority and infallibility, as well as that of individual conscience, came immediately under discussion: the Encyclical was a strong papal statement, issued by the Pope alone, against the advice of many cardinals and bishops.

Among the scholars who reacted within two weeks after the Encyclical was issued were: Hans Küng, Bernard Häring, and Karl Rahner (Germans); Charles Curran and 87 other American theologians, many from the Catholic University in Washington, D.C.; Gregory Baum (Austrian-born Canadian); Enda McDonagh (Ireland); Edward Schillebeeckx and a group of Dutch theologians; Philippe Delhaye and a group of Louvain-based professors (Delhaye himself a member of the Papal Commission); Jorge Mejia (Argentinian) and groups of Chilean, Brazilian, and Peruvian theologians; Marc Oraison (French theologian-psychiatrist); and a symposium of 20 European scholars meeting in Amsterdam. All stated that the Encyclical could be fallible as a matter of fact, and that the personal conscience of the married couple was the final authority on the subject. Delhaye asserted that the Encyclical was against the teaching of the Vatican Council on marriage; Küng said that Pope Paul had repeated the mistake made with Galileo Galilei.

Other theologians, admitting the Encyclical was not infallible, claimed that it still carried great authority and that the mind should give agreement and the will faith. They asserted that the Pope spoke not as an individual but as a representative of the Church; moreover, he spoke in regard to a teaching supported by Church tradition and affirmed by Pius XI and Pius XII. The representatives of the Church should not corrupt or weaken authority by open opposition, they stated. They concluded that conscience, guided by divine truth, has to arrive at the same conclusion as the Encyclical. This opinion was expressed by Roman theologians, like Gagnebet, Guzzetti, Bishop Colombo (the Pope's theologian), the Swiss cardinal-theologian Journet, the French theologian Danielou, the German Von Hildebrand, the Dutch Malta, many Spanish theologians, the American review *Triumph*, and a considerable number of American seminary and university professors.

These theologians supporting the Pope represented what, until about 10 years ago, was the general teaching on the authority of encyclicals, and on marriage. The idea of the supratemporal truth and teaching of the Church had, for at least the last two hundred years, been attached to this doctrine, making it psychologically difficult to accept a change.

The dissenters objected to the fact that never in recent history had a pope issued a statement with so little support from the Church itself. They pointed to the Vatican Council, which they said had taken the first step toward a more personalistic conception of marriage and responsible parenthood. And they noted many completely new developments—the demographic explosion, changed male-female relationships, technology, and a more optimistic concept of sexuality—which had changed the world in a short time. John Noonan, author of *Contraception, A History of Its Treatment by the Catholic Theologians and Canonists*, had shown that in the past, rapid social change had led to changes in Church doctrine on such issues as slavery, religious freedom and usury.

The dissenters attacked the argumentation of the Encyclical. They cited a lack of biblical evidence supporting the document and the inappropriateness of the few biblical texts quoted in *Humanae Vitae*. In addition, they described the appeal to tradition as unfair, since only in the last two hundred years had the Church given much attention to sex problems, and only in the middle of the nineteenth century had Rome dealt with the problem of contraception.

The conservative response to this attack was that the Encyclical was not a typically christian one, but rather was based on natural law, on evidence from human nature. Thus, they added, the Encyclical was addressed not only to Roman Catholics but 'to all men of goodwill.'

The dialogue came to focus on such topics as nature and culture or technology; nature and person; and mutation of mankind. 'What is the point we are discussing: Are all contraceptives, and not only the pill, against nature: About 80 per cent of the theologians answer no; the other 20 per cent (hesitantly) yes. This means that the concept of "nature" is under discussion,' said Marc Oraison. 'This means,' he added, 'that biblical, or typically christian arguments are not central, but, as in the time of Galileo, a cosmology, a way to see things. As in Galileo's time the Church was compromised in confusing an outdated concept of the physical world with theology, so the Encyclical negates findings of modern anthropology.'

German philosophers Arntz and David and Dutch philosopher Van Melzen criticized *Humanae Vitae* for using an aristotelian-thomistic, biological, and impersonal concept of 'nature,' which had been abandoned since the Middle Ages. On this particular point, the 87 Washington theologians, the 20 European scholars who met at the Amsterdam symposium, and the philosophers and theologians of the University of Louvain were most insistent. 'In conscience we have to declare that we do not see the validity of a conception which considers biological laws of the process of procreation as a predominant and in itself valid law, in isolation from the total aim of marriage and the family,' said the Louvain group. German moral theologian, Franz Boeckle, stated that the concept of nature used in the Encyclical did not even correspond to the medieval idea of it, but rather to a positivistic and biologistic corruption of it. All these moral theologians agreed that contraceptives, morally 'neutral' in themselves, could be used in a bad and therefore, impersonal way. For them, a new christian morality should concentrate on other questions, rather than on the concept of nature. The pope, Barbara Ward said, should have written an Encyclical on love and human relationships—those being the most fundamental problems of the times.

The ecumenical point of view

Churches and religions throughout the world reacted in diverse ways: ideological divisions often did not coincide with religious borders.

The Pope received approval from a number of non-Catholics, among them a group of Lutheran doctors from Ulm, Germany, and a number of Scandinavian Lutherans; Rajmoham Gandhi, the nephew of Mahatma Gandhi; a group of Moslems living in France led by Mohammed Cherif Zeghoudi; Fred Corson, ex-president of the World Methodist Council; the orthodox Jewish leader in Jerusalem; some professors of the El Ahram University in Cairo; and a group of Hindu leaders from the University of Benares in India. The main point of all these groups was that the Pope had the courage to take a stand against hedonism and the conception of sex as salvation. Another point raised in a number of reactions—e.g., from humanist organizations and members of Moral Rearmament—was that the Pope had taken a firm stand against 'manipulation of mankind by chemical means.'

An analysis of the religious point of view shows that favorable reactions came from the most 'orthodox' groups: high-church Lutherans and Anglicans; orthodox Calvinists; and orthodox Jews, Moslems, and Hindus.

The Eastern Orthodox churches were approving. Athenagoras I, Patriarch of Constantinople and a friend of Paul VI, stated: 'I am completely agreeing with the Pope. Paul VI could not have pronounced in any other way. The interests and the very existence of families and nations is at stake.' Nikodim, Russian Metropolitan of Leningrad, reacted in a similar way, as did the Greek Orthodox Church.

The negative reactions ranged from polite to aggressive, but did not basically differ from the Roman Catholic criticism. The issues contested included the concept of the immutability of truth, the unhistoricity of the Church, the concept of nature, the impersonal view of marriage, and the lack of biblical foundation.

It appears to some that the Encyclical has not harmed the ecumenical movement. 'It is a delusion for many christians in all the member churches of the World Council of Churches, as it is for many Roman Catholics, that there seems to be no progress towards a solution of this problem of conscience,' said Dr. Carson Blake, Secretary General of the World Council of Churches. The same delusion was also referred to by the Archbishop of Canterbury, Dr. Michael Ramsey, whose anglican communion had accepted the principle of artificial contraception at the 1958 Lambeth Conference. At a press conference given in the office of the International Documentation Center in Rome, Dr. Albert van den Heuvel, head of the communications department of the World Council of Churches, stated that the Encyclical would only hamper ecumenism in those circles where there was fear that the Roman Catholic Church had regressed to an intransigent and pre-Vatican II attitude.

The complexity of reactions to the Encyclical cannot be easily summarized. Uncertainty and discomfort prevail in this conflict of several forces: old, sometimes idealized, models of viewing the world; new, sometimes overly optimistic, approaches; and anxiety over the problems of the century and the future.

SOURCE: Population Council, *Studies in Family Planning* (February 1970)

22 Mrs Judith Hart
A WOMAN'S VIEW

To any man who says population control is a form of genocide, say: 'Ask any woman!'

Source: Mrs Judith Hart, former Minister of Overseas Development, UK

MARXISM

It is widely, but incorrectly, assumed that Marxism (or, variously, Communism and Socialism) is against family planning. The most practical and impressive evidence to the contrary is, of course, the experience of China (see p 75).

One paper which is of interest was that prepared by Prof B. Z. Urlanis, professor and doctor of economic sciences in the Soviet Union.

23 Professor B. Z. Urlanis
MARXISM AND BIRTH CONTROL

World literature widely expresses the view that Marxism does not recognise birth control and is opposed to its practice. In fact this is not so at all. Engels very clearly expressed himself on this question in his letter to Kautsky dated 1st February 1881. In this letter he wrote that 'if Communist society were ever forced to regulate the production of people . . . it could do so without difficulty.' Later on in that letter Engels reminded Kautsky that the process of birth regulation 'is already developed in France and Lower Austria.'* In another place Engels also took a positive view on birth control. He wrote, 'I still remain of the opinion that this is a private matter between husband and wife, and possibly their family doctor.'†

It is completely wrong to confuse questions of rationalising population growth with Malthusianism or neo-Malthusianism. The dissemination of definite medical knowledge about population cannot be regarded as neo-Malthusian propaganda. Already in 1913 V. I. Lenin published an article entitled 'The Working Class and Neo-Malthusianism' in which he made his position completely clear: 'The freedom of dissemination of medical knowledge and the defence of the elementary demo-

---

* Marx and Engels, *Works*, Vol. XXVII, p. 108.
† Marx and Engels, *Works*, Vol. XXVII, p. 281.

cratic rights of citizens of both sexes are one thing. The social teachings of neo-Malthusianism is something different.'*

1. The social meaning of neo-Malthusianism is to distract the workers from the struggle against exploitation and to persuade the proletariat that in order to improve its condition it must abandon the class struggle and find a solution for its difficult position in the small family system which could be achieved by a postponement of marriage. In the Malthusian view, an England containing eight million people, that is to say one-seventh of the present population, was already overpopulated; Malthus was for the elimination of all assistance to the poor and did his utmost to prove that the economic and political structure of capitalism had no responsibility for the poverty and the suffering of the people. In the political field, neo-Malthusians believed that the small family system was the answer to all social problems of modern society. That is the whole meaning of neo-Malthusianism about which Lenin wrote more than 50 years ago. Instead Marxists believe that although the limitation of family size among the working class has become widespread in capitalist countries, this in no way affects the intensity of the class struggle on the part of the proletariat.

2. The attitude of Marxism to birth control was clearly shown after the October revolution when the Bolshevik party took over the government of the country. Thus, abortions which were forbidden in Czarist Russia were legalised as far back as 1920. Naturally the aim of this legislation was not at all to limit the birth rate which in any case was relatively low at that time, but rather to give women the right themselves to determine whether they wished to become mothers depending on their conditions of life and work.

And nowadays women in the Soviet Union are free themselves to determine the number of children they wish to have. The sale of contraceptive appliances both male and female has never been prohibited in the Soviet Union, and the law authorises abortions for other than medical reasons.

* V. I. Lenin, *Works*, 5th edition, Vol. XXIII, p. 257.

It should not be concluded from all this that the Soviet Union wishes to lower its birth rate. On the contrary, a law enacted in 1944 provided for material help to large families.

What is fundamentally characteristic of the population policy of the Soviet Union is that women should be completely free to decide on the size of their families. Since most Soviet women are working women, and not just housewives, they must solve this question, taking into account their work situation and all the factors which are important for the rearing of their children.

Soviet women have wide social interests and a high cultural standard, and they therefore are not content to devote their best years to housework and the rearing of children. Although over eight million children are brought up in nurseries and kindergartens in the Soviet Union, a large number of children still stay with their mothers and thus hamper them in their working and social activities.

3. The high social position that women enjoy under socialism was brilliantly forecast by the leader of German Social Democracy, August Bebel. In his famous book entitled 'Woman and Socialism,' he wrote that: 'As regards the population question in the society of the future, decisive importance is assumed by the higher and more free position to be enjoyed by all women without exception. Intelligent and energetic women —we will not talk about exceptions—do not wish to have large numbers of children in accordance with "God's will" and to spend the best years of their lives in a state of pregnancy or with a child at the breast. This desire not to have too many children, which can already be seen among the majority of women, will increase in the future despite the help which Socialist society will give to pregnant women and mothers and in our view it is highly probable that in a socialist society the increase of population will be much lower than in a bourgeois society.'*

The trend towards small families is also due to the desire of

* A. Bebel, 'Woman and Socialism', M. 1959, pp. 577-578.

the parents to give their children the best conditions of life and the best education and not to spread their material resources over a large number of children.

As a result of all these factors birth control is in fact now practised almost throughout the whole of the Soviet Union; this means a responsible attitude on the part of parents to the formation of their family. Only in the central Asian Republics, in the Azerbaijan Soviet Socialist Republic, and in the Armenian Soviet Socialist Republic there is as yet no widespread birth control because of ethnic factors.

4. It is not difficult to calculate that given the present level of mortality and the fact that a certain percentage of people do not get married and because of involuntary childlessness on the part of some couples in order to replace the level of a generation, 100 married women must give birth during the whole of their lives to about 250 children. If families take the view that they want to have one or two children only, then even this will not ensure replacement. In our country therefore it is becoming necessary to follow a demographic policy that would encourage the births of second and third children.

The problem of the population policy is completely different in the developing countries, particularly in Asia, where a most unfavourable imbalance has arisen between the numbers of the population and the availability of resources. Of course the way out of this difficult situation is to increase the production of food through greater crop yields and planted acreage and through the industrialisation of the country. But Soviet demographers believe that together with an economic solution there must also be a demographic solution, that is to say, a lowering of birth rates by means of an effective demographic policy. The aim of such a policy must be to spread planned families, and this implies the use of birth control by the population.

5. Engels once said that men will consciously create their own history. This observation fully applies to the formation of the family. The birth of children should also be approached consciously and not be left to chance.

Natural fertility, i.e., rates determined solely by physiological fecundity, should be regarded as an atavism, an inheritance of the past, a remnant of colonialism. Among peoples who have thrown off the fetters of imperialism and who have started a new life, the position of women is improved and a woman must be given the possibility of having the number of children she desires, that is, the number of children she would be in a position to bring up satisfactorily. That means planned fertility which should spread throughout the world. This, of course, requires a large increase in educational standards and, above all, the liquidation of illiteracy, and it is precisely in this direction that governments of the newly independent countries should direct their efforts. Engels wrote that only the enlightenment of the masses would make it possible 'morally to limit the instinct of reproduction.'

At the same time the population problems of the developing countries, which are now causing concern to the entire world, should be settled with the help of economic demography. It is precisely that branch of demography which can study the question of the effect of the various generations on the national economy. Each man is a consumer for the duration of his natural life, and for the duration of his economically active life he is a producer. It is possible to find quantitative expressions for the total amounts he produces on one hand, and the total value of his consumption on the other, using the different categories of national income analysis and its distribution between consumption and investment.

6. In the case of many developing countries it may be assumed that if conditions of underemployment persist many generations may complete their lives, so that their consumption exceeds the amounts they have produced. The existence of such a negative balance depresses the economy of the countries in question and prevents improvements in the standard of living of their populations. In these conditions rapid population growth is a millstone around the neck of the developing countries. While using their own resources to the maximum they

also at the same time require assistance from the economically developed countries. The Soviet Union is giving very wide assistance to these countries. The Aswan Dam (U.A.R.) and the metallurgical complex at Bhilai (India) are striking illustrations of this policy. Over 100 educational and medical establishments and research centres are being built in African and Asian countries with the help of Soviet experts.

By using the help of the Soviet Union and other economically developed countries of the world, and on the basis of economic and social reforms which play a decisive role in raising these countries to higher levels by liquidating the remaining vestiges of colonial exploitation, and at the same time implementing thoroughly considered and well financed measures designed to spread planned families, the countries of Asia, Africa and Latin America may overcome the serious economic difficulties they are now experiencing and conquer hunger and malnutrition and ensure for their peoples a life worthy of the noble status of man.

A French writer once said that if mankind ever decided to build a palace of happiness, the largest room in such a palace would be the waiting room! Unfortunately some nations of the 'Third World' have already spent too long in this waiting room. The task of the demographer is to help peoples build a palace large enough to contain all men.

Summary
The idea widely spread in world literature that Marxism does not acknowledge birth control is completely untrue. Such an idea is denied by direct and indirect statements made on this question by Marx, Engels and Lenin.

Birth control is almost universally practised in the Soviet Union.

SOURCE: Population Council, *Studies in Family Planning* (January 1970)

ISLAM

A good deal of material has been collected on the Muslim viewpoint of family planning. Constant references are made to the Quran and the Hadith that restriction of the number of children has at no time been forbidden; in fact under certain circumstances it has been encouraged. There follows the Fatwa—or 'opinion'—of the Grand Mufti of Jordan on this subject.

24A Sheikh Abdullah Al-Qalqili
FATWA: FAMILY PLANNING IN ISLAM

In the name of God, The Merciful and the Compassionate. Fears of the world from the increase of population have assumed serious proportions everywhere, and experts have come to regard this as a portent of woe, ruination and dire consequences. In their consideration how the world can be protected against this towering evil and grave menace, they have been led to think that 'restriction of procreation' is one of the greatest measures. They know, however, that most people do not follow this course unless the ruling of religion, in this respect, has been made clear to them. Therefore, Muslims have looked up to reliable religious divines to state to them the ruling of religion on the subject. Questions converged on us for this purpose, including questions from official sources. This is our statement on this matter.

It is acknowledged that the liberal Islamic law accommodates itself to nature and to human conditions. God says: 'Set thou thy face then, as a true convert, towards the faith—the nature made by God in which he has made men; there is no altering of God's creation'.

One of the natural things inherent in human beings is marriage. But the purpose of marriage is procreation for the perpetuation of the species. The divine koranic verse refers to that, and regards it as one of the blessings bestowed upon God's servants. God says: 'God, too, has given you wives from among yourselves and has given you sons and grandsons from your wives, and supplied you with good things'. Therefore, marriage has been one of the Islamic religious ways and procreation has been one of its desirable and gratifying aims. Even the lawgiver views multiplicity with favour, for multiplicity implies power, influence and invulnerability. This is why, in one of the traditions of the Prophet, marriage with an affectionate prolific woman is strongly urged. The tradition says: 'Marry the affectionate prolific women, for I shall be proud of you among the nations'.

Nevertheless, the lawgiver made marriage with a prolific woman and marriage for procreation conditional upon the availability of means and the ability to bear the costs of marriage and to meet the expenses of child education and training, so that the children may not fall into bad company and develop anti-social ways. And according to the Islamic religious rule (laws change as conditions change), marriage should be disallowed if the would-be husband is incapable of meeting the expenses of married life. To this, reference is clear in the Koran and in the Traditions. The Koran says: 'And let those who do not find a match live in continence until God makes them free from want out of his bounty.' The Tradition says: 'O young men, whoever of you is capable, financially, let him marry, and whoever is not capable let him fast, for fasting is a preventive.' From the foregoing verse and the tradition, the definite inference is that 'restriction of procreation' is legal a fortiori; because to stop procreation altogether is more serious than to limit it. It is a cause for much wonder that those who urge celibacy should at the same time hesitate to allow family planning.

Moreover, there are genuine traditions which allow methods for restricting procreation, such as coitus interruptus. For instance, in the two most reliable collections of traditions, Abu-Said is reported to have said that in one of the raids, he and others captured a number of women, and they used to practise coitus interruptus. He also said that they asked the Prophet about that and the Prophet said: 'Indeed, do that,' and repeated it three times, and continued: 'No creature to be created from now till the Day of Judgement will not but be created'. Another report has it that a man said to the Prophet: 'I have a young wife, I hate that she should be pregnant, and I want what men want; but the Jews claim that coitus interruptus is minor infanticide.' The Prophet replied, 'The Jews lie. If God wishes to create the child, you will not be able to divert him from that'. In the two reliable collections of traditions, it is stated that Muslims used to practise coitus interruptus during the life-time of the Prophet and during the period of the Koranic revelation. It is also reliably reported that Muslims used to practise coitus interruptus during the lifetime of the Prophet, the Prophet knew of this, but he did not prohibit it.

In these genuine traditions there is definitely permission for the practice of coitus interruptus which is one of the ways of contraception or for restricting procreation even without excuse. Permission for this practice was reported by a number of the Prophet's Companions and Companions of the Companions, as laid down in the Four Orthodox Ways. A corollary of this is the dispensation for the use of medicine for contraception, or even for abortion before the embryo or the foetus is animated. The Hanafie allow that reason.

The jurists gave examples to illustrate the meaning of the excuse for abortion, as in Ibu Abidin who says: 'Like the mother who has a baby still unweaned and who becomes pregnant and thus her milk ceases, and the father is unable to hire a wet nurse to save the life of his baby.'

The Jurists also state that it is permissible to make medicine for abortion so long as the embryo is still unformed in the human shape. The period of this unformed state is given as 120 days. The jurists think that during this period the embryo or the foetus is not yet a human being. A report says that Omar (The Second Caliph) does not regard abortion as infanticide unless the foetus is already past the limit.

Milik, the founder of the Miliki Orthodox Way, says that the husband should not practise coitus interruptus with his wife unless she permits it. Alzarqani, in his comment on this, says that the practice is lawful if the wife allows it. Permission or prohibition of coitus interruptus may serve as a guide in deciding the question of abortion before the foetus is animated.

All this shows that there is agreement among the founders of the four Orthodox Ways that coitus interruptus is allowed as a means of contraception. Religious savants inferred from this that contraceptives might be used, and even medicines might be used for abortion.

Accordingly, we hereby give our judgement with confidence in favour of family planning.

SOURCE: Abdullah Al-Qalqili, 'Family Planning in Islam', Statement (December 1964), mimeo issued by the International Planned Parenthood Federation

The following passage comes from a report of a conference held at Rabat, Morocco, in December 1971. It may be noted that opinion was against both sterilisation and abortion.

24B Rabat Conference
ON FAMILY PLANNING

A conference of 80 eminent Muslim specialists and scholars of jurisprudence, medical sciences, sociology, philosophy, history, political science, economy and demography, from 24 countries representing various Islamic sects, was convened by the Middle East and North African Region of the International Planned Parenthood Federation in Rabat, Morocco, at the end of December. The conference examined the attitude of Islam towards the social changes facing the Muslim family and its stand about the issues of family planning, abortion and sterilization.

Forty-four research papers on these subjects were read at the conference and fully discussed and debated by the delegates. Subsequently the following statement was issued:

'Being fully convinced that Islam has comprehensive legislation providing for all necessary steps leading to the creation of a completely integrated and happy family as the foundation unit of a Muslim society which is to be coherent and firmly established; and in pious fulfilment of the momentous task required of the members of the conference, with a balanced view as to the provisions of Sharia and the spirit of religious legislation, in the light of scientific facts, the conference has formed the following views:

(1) The Sharia, consisting as it is of regulations for family life, has sufficient provision for complete security and order within the family as a safeguard against its disintegration and the weakening of its structure.

(2) The Sharia, both as explicitly provided in the texts of the Holy Qur'an and the traditions and as deduced from other sources in accordance with the strict rules of Islamic methods of discretion, ensures for the Muslim family the ways to meet the challenge of new situations and to find the proper solutions serving the welfare of the family.

(3) The Sharia allows the Muslim family the necessary latitude for enabling it to regulate its life in such a way or ways as would lead to balanced procreation either for increasing or decreasing its size, and for helping parents to overcome the handicap of sterility and for spacing the incidence of pregnancy, making use in all such cases of safe and legitimate methods of contraception.

(4) The question of sterilization was fully discussed by the conference and the trend was to adopt the findings of the Islamic Research Council in Al-Azhar regarding this matter, namely that the use of sterilization methods are against Islam and must not be practised either by the parents or by any others.

(5) On the problem of abortion as a means for getting rid of the foetus, the conference maintains that all Muslim savants are unanimously agreed that after the fourth month of pregnancy abortion is strictly prohibited unless it is for saving the

mother's life. But with regard to abortion during the period prior to the end of the fourth month it has been pointed out that views of competent religious authorities on the subject are varied. Nevertheless, the conference considers that the sound view is in the direction of prohibiting it at any stage of pregnancy, except in the extreme case where the life of the mother must be safeguarded.

And it is to God that we turn for guidance.'

SOURCE: *International Planned Parenthood News* (February 1972)

The late President Nasser, however, realised the dangers to Egypt of uncontrolled population increase.

'The population increase constitutes the most dangerous obstacle that faces the Egyptian people in their drive towards raising the standards of production in their country in an effective and efficient way.'

SOURCE: Gamal Abdel Nasser, President, United Arab Republic

PART FIVE

Organisations Concerned with Population Problems

UNITED NATIONS

The major organisation concerned with population problems is the United Nations, and its involvement reflects the high priority the nations of the world are giving to population research and limitation.

25A UN
STATEMENT OF POLICY ON POPULATION

Population problems and policies are major areas of concern to the United Nations. Advice and assistance are provided in particular on policy development, on the development of national programmes related to economic and social development plans, on demographic statistics and research needed for economic and social planning and on training of personnel. A number of the United Nations bodies are involved in various aspects of population, including the General Assembly, the Economic and Social Council and its Committee for Programme and Co-ordination, the Population Commission, the Statistical Commission, the Commission for Social Development, the Commission on the Status of Women, the Committee on Development Planning, the Advisory Committee on the Application of Science and Technology to Development and the regional economic commissions.

The main objective of the United Nations programme of research related to fertility is to increase the knowledge and understanding of fertility levels and trends and factors affecting them, especially in developing countries.

The training of demographers in substantive and selective technical aspects of fertility and related aspects of family planning programmes forms an essential part of the programmes of the regional demographic training and research centres sponsored by the United Nations.

Improvement of demographic statistics is carried out through programmes designed for this purpose having two distinct facets: collection, evaluation and publication of national statistics in an international format, and the provision of technical assistance to countries upon request.

The technical assistance activities of the United Nations in the field of human fertility and related fields cover many diverse aspects including assistance in vital statistics and population census-taking; analyses of fertility levels and trends, and the study of their economic and social implications; studies aimed at contributing to the formulation of national population policies regarding fertility; and evaluation of various aspects of national family planning programmes.

The Commission for Social Development has for a long time been dealing with social questions related to population, including the development and utilization of human resources.

All the regional economic commissions, the Economic and Social Office in Beirut and the Division of Social Affairs at Geneva have mandates in, and carry out activities on, population as related to their regions in accordance with the over-all mandate of the United Nations.

SOURCE: UN, New York

The 1954 and 1965 World Population Conferences were held under UN auspices, and in 1966 the General Assembly adopted a historic resolution that provided for direct involvement of the whole UN system in the field of population.

25B UN
RESOLUTION ON POPULATION

2211 [XXI]. Population growth and economic development

The General Assembly

Recalling its resolution 1838 (XVII) of 18 December 1962 on population growth and economic development and Economic and Social Council resolutions 933 C (XXXV) of 5 April 1963 on the intensification of demographic studies, research and training, 1048 (XXXVII) of 15 August 1964 on population growth and economic and social development and 1084 (XXXIX) of 30 July 1965 on work programmes and priorities in the field of population,

Recalling World Health Assembly resolutions WHA 18.49 of 21 May 1965 and WHA 19.43 of 20 May 1966 on the health aspects of world population,

Taking note of resolution 3.252 adopted on 29 November 1966 by the General Conference of the United Nations Educational, Scientific and Cultural Organization at its fourteenth session, and of paragraphs 842-844 of the programme for 1967-1968 of that organization on the subject of education and information related to population growth,

Recalling the inquiry conducted by the Secretary-General among Governments on problems resulting from the interaction of economic growth and population change, and his report thereon, which reflected a wide variety of population problems,

Commending the Economic and Social Council and the Secretary-General for convening the World Population Conference, held at Belgrade from 30 August to 10 September 1965, in which a large number of specialists in demography and related fields from developing countries were able to participate,

Taking note of the summary of the highlights of the World Population Conference,

Noting the steps taken by the organizations of the United Nations system concerned to co-ordinate their work in the field of population,

Concerned at the growing food shortage in the developing countries, which is due in many cases to a decline in the production of food-stuffs relative to population growth,

Recognizing the need for further study of the implications of the growth, structure and geographical distribution of population for economic and social development, including national health, nutrition, education and social welfare programmes carried out at all levels of government activity,

Believing that demographic problems require the consideration of economic, social, cultural, psychological and health factors in their proper perspective,

Recognizing the sovereignty of nations in formulating and promoting their own population policies, with due regard to the principle that the size of the family should be the free choice of each individual family,

1. *Invites* the Economic and Social Council, the Population Commission, the regional economic commissions, the United Nations Economic and Social Office in Beirut and the specialised agencies concerned to study the proceedings of the 1965 World Population Conference when pursuing their activities in the field of population;

2. *Notes with satisfaction* the decision of the World Health Organization to include in its programme of activities the study of the health aspects of human reproduction and the provision of advisory services, upon request, within its responsibilities under World Health Assembly resolution WHA 19.43, and the decision of the United Nations Educational, Scientific and Cultural Organization to stimulate and provide assistance towards scientific studies concerning the relations between the development of education and population;

3. *Requests* the Secretary-General:

(a) To pursue, within the limits of available resources, the implementation of the work programme covering training, research, information and advisory services in the field of population in the light of the recommendations of the Population Commission contained in the report on its thirteenth session, as endorsed by the Economic and Social Council in its resolution 1084 (XXXIX), and of the considerations set forth in the preamble of the present resolution;

(b) To continue his consultations with the specialized agencies concerned, in order to ensure that the activities of the United Nations system of organizations in the field of population are effectively co-ordinated;

(c) To present to the Population Commission at its fourteenth session, as envisaged in Economic and Social Council resolution 1084 (XXXIX), proposals with regard to the priorities of work over periods of two and five years, within the framework of the long-range programme of work in the field of population;

4. *Calls upon* the Economic and Social Council, the Population Commission, the regional economic commissions, the United Nations Economic and Social Office in Beirut and the specialized agencies concerned to assist, when requested, in further developing and strengthening national and regional facilities for training, research, information and advisory services in the field of population, bearing in mind the different character of population problems in each country and region and the needs arising therefrom.

1497th plenary meeting,
17 December 1966.

SOURCE: General Assembly resolution 2211 (XXI) (1966)

U Thant, the former Secretary-General of the UN, has said: 'The most urgent conflict confronting the world of today is not between nations or ideologies, but between the pace of growth of the human race and the insufficient increase in resources needed to support mankind in peace, prosperity and dignity'.

On Human Rights Day, 10 December 1966, he issued a Declaration on Population developed on the initiative of John D. Rockefeller 3rd, Chairman of the Board, Population Council (see p 209), and signed by the heads of state of twelve countries. A year later, eighteen other heads of state had added their names to the document. This document is of historic importance in setting the stage for international recognition of the urgency of the population problem.

25C UN
STATEMENT BY HEADS OF STATE

The peace of the world is of paramount importance to the community of nations, and our governments are devoting their best efforts to improving the prospects for peace in this and succeeding generations. But another great problem threatens the world—a problem less visible but no less immediate. That is the problem of unplanned population growth.

It took mankind all of recorded time until the middle of the last century to achieve a population of one billion. Yet it took less than a hundred years to add the second billion, and only thirty years to add the third. At today's rate of increase, there will be four billion people by 1975 and nearly seven billion people by the year 2000. This unprecedented increase presents us with a situation unique in human affairs and a problem that grows more urgent with each passing day.

The numbers themselves are striking, but their implications are of far greater significance. Too rapid population growth seriously hampers efforts to raise living standards, to further education, to improve health and sanitation, to provide better housing and transportation, to forward cultural and recreational opportunities—and even in some countries to assure sufficient food. In short, the human aspiration, common to men everywhere, to live a better life is being frustrated and jeopardized.

As heads of governments actively concerned with the population problem, we share these convictions:

We believe that the population problem must be recognized

ORGANISATIONS CONCERNED WITH POPULATION PROBLEMS 175

as a principal element in long-range national planning if governments are to achieve their economic goals and fulfill the aspirations of their people.

We believe that the great majority of parents desire to have the knowledge and the means to plan their families; that the opportunity to decide the number and spacing of children is a basic human right.

We believe that lasting and meaningful peace will depend to a considerable measure upon how the challenge of population growth is met.

We believe the objective of family planning is the enrichment of human life, not its restriction; that family planning, by assuring greater opportunity to each person, frees man to attain his individual dignity and reach his full potential.

Recognizing that family planning is in the vital interest of both the nation and the family, we, the undersigned, earnestly hope that leaders around the world will share our views and join with us in this great challenge for the well being and happiness of people everywhere.

HAROLD HOLT, *Prime Minister of Australia*
ERROL W. BARROW, *Prime Minister of Barbados*
DR. CARLOS LLERAS RESTREPO, *President of Colombia*
JENS OTTO KRAG, *Prime Minister of Denmark*
DR. JOAQUIN BALAGUER, *President of Dominican Republic*
DR. D. URHO KEKKONEN, *President of Finland*
LT. GEN. J. A. ANKRAH, *Chairman of the National Liberation Council of Ghana*
MME. INDIRA GANDHI, *Prime Minister of India*
GENERAL SUHARTO, *Acting President of Indonesia*
SHAH MOHAMMAD REZA PAHLAVI, *Emperor of Iran*
EISAKO SATO, *Prime Minister of Japan*
HIS MAJESTY HUSSEIN, *King of Hashemite Kingdom of Jordan*
GENERAL CHUNG HEE PARK, *President of Republic of Korea*
TUNKU ABDUL RAHMAN, *Prime Minister of Malaysia*
HIS MAJESTY HASSAN II, *King of Morocco*

His Majesty Mahendra, *King of Nepal*
Dr. J. Zijlstra, *Prime Minister of The Netherlands*
Keith Holyoake, *Prime Minister of New Zealand*
Per Borten, *Prime Minister of Norway*
Field Marshal Mohammed Ayub Khan, *President of Pakistan*
Ferdinand E. Marcos, *President of Republic of the Philippines*
Lee Kwan Yew, *Prime Minister of Singapore*
Tage Erlander, *Prime Minister of Sweden*
Thanom Kittikachorn, *Prime Minister of Thailand*
Eric Williams, *Prime Minister of Trinidad and Tobago*
Habib Bourguiba, *President of Tunisia*
Gamal Abdel Nasser, *President of UAR*
Harold Wilson, *Prime Minister of United Kingdom*
Lyndon B. Johnson, *President of United States of America*
Marshal Josip Broz-Tito, *President of Yugoslavia*

Source: Population Council, *Studies in Family Planning*

The Proclamation of Teheran, which was the final testimony of the UN Human Rights Conference of April 1968, and the General Assembly's 1969 Declaration on Social Development both had important implications for the progress of work in the field of population. The International Development Strategy for the second United Nations development decade, adopted by the General Assembly in October 1970, provided for action at national and international levels to deal with the problem of population growth. The ID Strategy stated: 'Each developing country should formulate its own demographic objectives within the framework of its national development plan'.

The work of the United Nations received encouragement from President Richard M. Nixon in 1969.

26 President Richard M. Nixon
MESSAGE ON POPULATION

It is our belief that the United Nations, its specialized agencies, and other international bodies should take the leadership in responding to world population growth. The United States will cooperate fully with their programs. I would note in this connection that I am most impressed by the scope and thrust of the recent report of the Panel of the United Nations Association, chaired by John D. Rockefeller 3rd. The report stresses the need for expanded action and greater coordination, concerns which should be high on the agenda of the United Nations.

Source: Presidential Message on Population (18 July 1969)

The General Assembly at its 25th session passed a resolution designating 1974 as World Population Year. This historic act must be seen both as a culmination to a long process of concern and as the precursor of a new and vast commitment by the international community and by the nations and peoples of the world to the principle of population planning.

The harsh fact is that, even though awareness of the dimensions of the population problem has risen at an unprecedented rate over the past few years, the efforts which are presently being made to promote solutions to that problem remain ludicrously small when compared to the overwhelming need.

World Population Year has five main objectives:
1. *To improve knowledge of and information on the facts concerning population trends and prospects—in both developed and developing countries.*
2. *To sharpen awareness and to heighten appreciation of population problems and their implications by individual governments, by non-governmental organisations and by scientific institutions.*
3. *To promote effective education on population, family life and reproductive functions through formal and other educational systems.*
4. *To promote the consideration of demographic factors in development planning and the development of policies and programmes in population fields which individual governments might wish to undertake.*
5. *To expand international co-operation in population fields and to increase the supply of suitable technical assistance to countries which desire it, and in accordance with their needs.*

27A UN
WORLD POPULATION YEAR, 1974

The General Assembly,

Noting ... that the International Development Strategy for the Second United Nations Development Decade provides for action, both at the national and international levels, to deal with the problem of population growth in these countries which, in accordance with their concept of development, consider that their rate of population growth hampers their development ...

Recognizing that, in spite of the progress made so far in this regard by Member States and international organizations, and particularly the important role being played in the population field by the United Nations Fund for Population Activities, varied aspects of the population problem require further attention from Member States and international organizations.

Recognizing further that a way of focusing international attention on different aspects of the population problem would be for Member States and international organizations to devote the year 1974 especially to appropriate efforts and undertakings in the field of population in the context of their respective needs and areas of competence ...

1. Designates the year 1974 as World Population Year;

2. Acknowledges that the formulation and implementation of population policies and programmes are matters falling under the internal competence of each country and, consequently, that international action in the population sphere should be responsive to the varied needs and requests of individual Member States;

3. Requests the Secretary-General to prepare, in consultation with interested Member States, a detailed programme of proposed measures and activities to be undertaken by the organizations of the United Nations system during the year 1974, taking

into account the different character of population problems in each country and region, the population policies of Member States, as well as the proposals contained in the Secretary-General's report on the question of holding a third World Population Conference, and to submit the programme to the Economic and Social Council in 1972 through the Population Commission at its sixteenth session;

4. Invites interested organizations of the United Nations system to render the necessary assistance to the Secretary-General in preparing the programme of measures and activities for the World Population Year;

5. Invites Member States to participate fully in the World Population Year in the context of their capacities and policies;

6. Stresses that assistance from organizations of the United Nations system and interested Member States should continue to be available upon request for evolving and implementing a dynamic population policy to cope with all the problems emanating from different population levels, characteristics and trends, including assistance in developing a comprehensive demographic research and studies programme as well as training programmes, and in providing advisory services in this field...

SOURCE: General Assembly resolution 2626 (XXV) (December 1970)

The highlight of the year will be the World Population Conference, which will bring together government leaders and international specialists to study and exchange views on population issues and to examine a draft World Population Plan of Action being formulated by the Secretary-General with the assistance of an Advisory Committee of Experts on Global Population Strategy.

27B UN RECOMMENDATION FOR WORLD POPULATION PLAN OF ACTION

GOAL While the precise formulation of demographic goals will remain a matter for each individual nation,
—countries in which rapid population growth is now occurring should consider seeking to reduce their rates of natural increase to less than 1·5 per cent a year over the next two decades,
—relatively low fertility countries that are already growing more slowly than this should seek to approach more closely a stationary population level over the next 20 years.

SOURCE: Report of US National Academy of Sciences on Rapid Population Growth (1972)

It has been estimated that the total development expenditures required during the Second Development Decade for intensified population programmes might be between $10 to $13 thousand million for the decade as a whole. The approximate total estimated costs of the potential contribution of the United Nations system in the field of population is estimated at $700 million for the Decade. That is a measure of the scale of the need.

28 Philip M. Hauser
THE POPULATION DILEMMA

The basic question before the developing nations of the world is whether family size can change before other basic cultural and social changes have transformed the values and goals of their peoples. Certainly the stakes involved are so high that every effort to reduce the birth rate—even in regions that are still mainly traditional peasant societies mired in poverty and illiteracy—is greatly desirable. But it must be recognized that up to this point in human history there has yet to emerge the first example of a population characterized by traditionalism, illiteracy and poverty that has managed to reduce its birth rate.

SOURCE: Philip M. Hauser, *The Population Dilemma* (1969)

United Nations Fund for Population Activities

29 UN
THE WORK OF UNFPA

The United Nations Fund for Population Activities (the Population Fund) was created by the Secretary-General in 1967 to assist developing countries with high population growth rates and low national incomes to solve their population problems, to expand the population activities of the United Nations system as a whole, and to pursue new and innovative programmes in this hitherto sadly neglected field.

This action was taken in response to resolutions in the Economic and Social Council in July 1965 and the General Assembly in December 1966, sponsored by a handful of countries alarmed at the rate at which the peoples of the world were using up the earth's resources. Governments, institutions and individuals were thus given the opportunity of making voluntary contributions to add international impetus to national population efforts.

But it was still not a priority effort for many nations. A few years later, in December 1971, the General Assembly, with 94 votes for, 20 abstentions and no opposition, passed a resolution recognizing the Population Fund as the focal point of the population efforts of the UN system and giving it a leadership role in promoting and co-ordinating international population programmes.

The relationship between population growth and economic and social progress has long been recognized by the United

Nations and taken into account by agencies providing assistance to developing countries. The Population Division of the United Nations, in particular, is one of the world's most reliable sources of the demographic information needed by all nations for successful development planning.

The advent of the Fund, however, has not only increased the size and scope of the population work of the United Nations system but also widened its sphere of influence by encouraging greater coordination between United Nations supported activities and those of bilateral, non-governmental and private organizations.

Briefly, the Population Fund assists national efforts by:

—promoting government awareness of social and economic implications of population problems;

—providing systematic and sustained assistance to countries seeking to define and solve population problems;

—helping organizations within the UN system to be more effective and efficient in planning, programming and implementing population projects supported by the Fund;

—assuming a leadership role in developing populaion strategies.

The Population Fund aids all aspects of population work and the projects supported cover a wide range of activities including: collection and analysis of basic demographic data; provision of demographic research and training facilities; demonstration programmes in family planning connected with maternal and child welfare services; inclusion of courses on population subjects in such educational programmes as adult education, teacher training and agricultural extension; provision of fellowships in the fields of population statistics, census-taking, demography, health education, human reproduction, communications evaluation and public administration; provision of contraceptive supplies and manufacturing materials, if requested, and formulation of population policies and the measures to be taken in accordance with national development objectives.

Global approach
By mid-1972 the Fund was financing over 500 projects benefitting 74 countries and developing areas. Of these, many were regional and inter-regional activities and included staff support to population units within the United Nations Economic Commissions of the respective regions. The Economic Commissions play an important part in helping their member states to formulate population policies and implement population programmes.

In Africa, for example, where many countries are virtually without census-based statistics, the first priority is to ascertain population trends and obtain overall demographic information. Under the sponsorship of the Economic Commission for Africa (ECA), an African Census Programme has been launched to provide not only information on the current structure of population but also on the dynamics of population. Twenty out of 41 members of ECA have already started demographic programmes and the rest are preparing to do so. It is estimated that the Fund will provide at least $11 million over a three-year period for censuses and national demographic surveys. The Fund also supports a regional demographic centre in Cameroon for French-speaking nations, and one for English-speaking countries in Ghana.

In Asia and the Far East, where the relationship between population and national advancement is well understood, most countries have already embarked on vigorous population programmes. At the regional level, most of the projects being aided by the Fund are devoted to training, education and research.

Among the top-priority activities are a research and action Programme concerning population and employment; a project to improve the facilities of the Asian Trade Union College, which is the only trade union workers' education body in Asia; a clearing house and curriculum materials centre in population education; and a medical documentation and production centre with special reference to family planning.

The Asian Press Foundation is receiving assistance to increase the services of 'DEPTHnews', a news agency covering development economics and population, to train local journalists in population and development reporting, and to provide a reference system for newspapers. The Population Division of the Economic Commission for Asia and the Far East (ECAFE) in addition to conducting extensive demographic activities also exercises a coordinating function in regard to population activities in the region.

In the Middle East, establishment of a population unit within the United Nations Economic and Social Office in Beirut (UNESOB) marked the beginning of rapidly expanding population programmes. This is the direct result of expert reports and studies made by UNESOB which have revealed urgent needs for help in carrying out comprehensive censuses in many countries, in solving specific problems associated with nomadic societies, in coping with changes brought about by rising rates of urbanization and in determining the underlying causes of the universally high population growth rates in Islamic countries. Among the training and research projects now being supported by the Fund are special courses in demography at the Kuwait Institute of Economic and Social Planning, a Population Study and Research Unit at the National Institute of Social Sciences of the Lebanese University and at the Cairo Demographic Centre. A special mission is also examining the possibilities of establishing an Inter-regional Population Research and Study Centre at Al-Azhar University in Egypt to provide multi-disciplinary training, undertake applied and operational research, and disseminate information in the population field. Al-Azhar has a student body of over 30,000, representative of 70 different nationalities from Moslem communities all over the world.

In Latin America, CELADE, the regional Demographic centre located in Santiago, Chile, has provided demographic training, information and advisory services for the benefit of its member countries over a period of years. Fund assistance has been given to expand the Centre's facilities and to finance such special projects as exchange programmes in teaching and research in the social sciences, as well as training courses in the evaluation of family planning programmes. As a result of strong religious and cultural attitudes, however, family planning programmes, where they exist at all, have usually been carried out by private organizations. Only a few countries, mainly in Central America and the Caribbean, have received aid from the Fund to support government-sponsored programmes. The decision of the Government of Chile in 1972, to engage in a nation-wide family health programme with assistance from the Fund, followed by an announcement by the Government of Mexico of the launching of a major programme are clear indications of new thinking and policies which may well affect other countries in the region.

New trend

An important development in the Fund's programming is the movement away from small projects handled regionally and inter-regionally to more comprehensive country projects. This trend results from increasing government awareness of the interdependent nature of population work.

Cost of projects approved by the Population Fund (by year, region and sector)

Totals:
1970	$ 6,700,000
1971	*15,300,000
1972 (estimate)	44,660,000
1972–75 (Four Year Work Plan)	254,000,000

1971 Expenditures by Region
Africa	$ 1,800,000
Asia and the Far East	5,800,000
Near and Middle East	2,000,000
Latin America	2,000,000
Inter-regional	3,700,000
	*$ 15,300,000

* Before year-end adjustments.

1972 Expenditures by Sector

	Estimated Costs
BASIC POPULATION DATA (Censuses, vital statistics, sample surveys, other statistics)	$ 6,905,000
POPULATION DYNAMICS (Research projects, training & research facilities, population aspects of planning)	5,615,000
POPULATION POLICY (Policy formulation, including conferences and seminars, and implementation, exclusive of family planning programmes)	1,255,000
FAMILY PLANNING (Delivery systems, programme management, fertility regulation techniques)	20,660,000
COMMUNICATION AND EDUCATION (For motivation in family planning)	3,960,000
MULTI-SECTOR ACTIVITIES (Fellowships, documentation centres, support to non-UN organizations, preparation of World Population Year)	2,230,000
FIELD STAFF, INFRA-STRUCTURE, OVERHEAD.	4,035,000
TOTAL	$ 44,660,000

Major country projects

In the Arab Republic of Egypt, a country covered by vast deserts, 35 million people have only 2·6% of the land area on which to grow food. With a growth rate of 28 per thousand, even optimistic projections set the population figure at 70 million in 1995—unless fertility declines substantially. The Government recognized the serious problem as far back as 1962 and established a national family planning programme. The UNFPA stepped in with advisers on population programmes and contraceptive supplies and, more recently, under an agreement operative since October 1971, the Fund is providing $1·25 million for the first year of a five-year programme of support for public information, education, study of population trends, research, fellowships and further supply of contraceptives through UNICEF.

Ten year target

India, which boasts the oldest government-sponsored family planning programme in the world, is trying to improve the effectiveness of the programme, which still reaches only a fraction of the population. The aim is to reduce the growth rate from 25 to 15 per thousand in the next decade. In 1969, India asked the United Nations to evaluate the programme, and the immediate result was a substantial increase in government expenditures and in bilateral support. The Fund, for its part, has agreed to contribute $1 million for an innovative vasectomy campaign; it also has supported a Demographic Training Centre in Bombay as well as educational projects.

Unique agreement

Maldistribution of the population in Indonesia is a major problem—60 per cent of the population is concentrated on three small islands, Bali, Java and Madura. The country has a population of 121 million and an annual growth rate of 26 per thousand. Early in 1972, the Government, aware that a major effort was necessary to change the adverse trend, entered into a unique cooperative agreement with the Fund and the World Bank at a total cost of $33 million. It provides for construction of schools, headquarters and other facilities for family planning services, and for training of personnel and assistance with communications research and evaluation programmes.

New targets

Rapidly decreasing water resources in Iran, coupled with disproportionate distribution of population, moved the Government to set new targets in an effort to reduce population growth. The Fund became involved at an early stage, providing consultants in demography and also a high-level evaluation mission whose recommendations have been adopted. Under a 17-month agreement signed in 1971, it is providing $1,630,000 in aid of the Iranian family planning programme. Support is now being given to training, research, communications, improvement of census-taking and to three maternity hospitals.

Intolerable crowding
Although the present population of Mauritius is only 800,000, population trends could lead to a doubling of the population by the year 2000 and an intolerable crowding situation. Consequently, the Government in 1970 signed a three-year agreement with the Fund totalling $600,000. It is designed to enable the local Ministry of Health to take over maternal and health services, reorganize and expand them and build in family planning components. Until now, these services had been provided by private organizations. WHO is recruiting advisers to assist the Ministry, and UNICEF is arranging for supply of contraceptives.

Family planning
Forty million people live in the Philippines, which has one of the highest growth rates (3·4 percent annually) in the world. The spectre of a population of nearly 100 million by the year 2000, with its pressure upon natural resources and social services, has prompted the Government to step up its family planning services. Early in 1972 the Fund increased and consolidated its assistance, committing $3·3 million for a five-year agreement supporting population education, teaching and training programmes in family planning as well as purchase of medical equipment.

Voluntary action
A doubled population by 1990 is the prospect for Thailand, which presently has 38 million inhabitants. In 1970, the Government launched a voluntary family planning programme which has since expanded to all 71 provinces. The Fund recently signed an agreement with Thailand, amounting to $3·2 million, to accelerate introduction of maternal and child health services, to support a family planning field workers

ORGANISATIONS CONCERNED WITH POPULATION PROBLEMS 189

project, and to develop communications activities and a voluntary sterilization programme. Fund support for Thailand is not new. In recent years, it funded family planning components in ongoing WHO and UNICEF programmes, involving health clinics, training of midwives, supplies and consultant services.

Leading the way
Chile is the first Latin-American country which concluded an agreement with the Fund, amounting to over $3 million for a four-year period. Under the terms of the agreement, signed in June, 1972, the Fund will support the family health and population programme, for which Chile has allocated $345 million of its own resources. The Fund's aid includes $1 million worth of contraceptive materials. Aim of the government programme is to reduce mortality, improve infant care and promote family welfare. An important feature in the Latin-American context is the decision to make birth control information available to all women regardless of marital status. So far, only 10 percent of Chile's women are covered by family planning programmes and the aim is to increase the coverage to 40 percent in the four-year period.

How it works
In 1969, when the Population Fund was in its early stages, the Secretary-General entrusted its overall supervision to the Administrator of the United Nations Development Programme (UNDP). Rafael M. Salas, former Cabinet Minister and Executive Secretary of the Philippines, was appointed Executive Director.

Close relationship with the UNDP—the world's largest source of pre-investment and technical assistance to low-income countries—enables the Fund to view the development picture as a whole in determining priorities for population activities and in directing aid to areas where it can do most good.

In deciding on programmes and directions for the Population

Fund, the Administrator and the Executive Director take into account advice and guidance of three consultative bodies—an Advisory Board, a United Nations Inter-Agency Consultative Committee and a Programme Consultative Committee.

Advisory Board, appointed by the Secretary-General, meets periodically to help formulate policies of the Population Fund and review performance of programmes and projects being supported. Members of the Board can also be consulted individually.

Inter-Agency Consultative Committee, major source of advice for the Fund, brings together representatives of the United Nations agencies and organizations which execute projects financed by the Fund or which run parallel programmes. Meetings provide opportunity for discussing programmes, policies and procedures and for co-ordinating Fund-supported projects.

Programme Consultative Committee ensures co-ordination with governmental agencies and private institutions in countries which contribute to the Fund, as well as with international organizations active in population. Meetings are attended by representatives of the Governments of Canada, Denmark, Egypt, Federal Republic of Germany, Finland, Indonesia, Iran, Japan, Kenya, Netherlands, Norway, Sweden, United Kingdom and United States, and by officials of British Overseas Development Administration (ODA), Canadian International Development Agency (CIDA), Swedish International Development Authority (SIDA), United States Agency for International Development (USAID), as well as private institutions such as Ford Foundation, Population Council, Rockefeller Foundation, Population Crisis Committee, and International Planned Parenthood Federation.

A key role

Resident Representatives, who head UNDP offices in the developing countries, play a key role in helping the Population Fund to meet its objectives. These officials assist governments in formulating requests for aid and in co-ordinating the work of all members of the UN family engaged in vital aspects of population programmes.

Resident Representatives help governments identify areas where population activities could best contribute to national development, inform the Fund of the overall pattern of assistance so that resources supplement, but do not compete with other efforts, and see that field operations are performed promptly and effectively. Requests for population project assistance from national, non-governmental organizations are also handled by the Resident Representative, who considers the merits of the request and also the standing of the requesting organization.

The Fund is now strengthening the Resident Representatives' staff with highly qualified personnel to help monitor and advise on population activities in the field.

Allocations issued to executing agencies for country, regional and inter-regional projects

	1971 only	Cumulative to 12/31/71
FAO	446,134	583,759
IBRD	400,000	400,000
ILO	285,253	609,983
IPPF	750,000	1,200,000
UN	5,013,391	8,903,399
UNDP	133,010	218,005
UNESCO	672,075	1,095,935
UNICEF	3,028,861	3,694,261
UNIDO	42,500	42,500
WHO	3,902,151	5,714,741
	14,673,375*	22,462,583

It is interesting to add that for the first half of 1972, allocations had already reached $17,277,802 and that cumulative allocations had totalled $39,740,385.

* After year-end adjustments.

The executing agencies

Responsibility for implementing projects financed by the Population Fund is assigned to various organizations according to their particular competencies.

Though most projects are carried out by member organizations of the United Nations system, the Fund may call on services of non-governmental organizations, if they are suited for particular tasks and if governments concerned do not object. These organizations include the International Planned Parenthood Federation (IPPF) and the Population Council.

United Nations organizations implementing projects are: United Nations (mainly the Population Division of the Secretariat), United Nations Children's Fund (UNICEF), Food and Agriculture Organization (FAO), International Labour Organization (ILO), United Nations Educational, Scientific and Cultural Organization (UNESCO), World Health Organization (WHO) and the United Nations Industrial Development Organization (UNIDO). Cooperative arrangements have also been made with the World Bank (IBRD) and the World Food Programme.

Increasingly, however, the Fund is providing aid for specific projects or events outside the agency structure. These include grants to: World Education Inc.; Press Foundation of Asia; World Assembly of Youth; International Council of Women; Law and Population Research Studies in several developing countries, including Lebanon, Ghana and Ethiopia; and International Youth Conference on Human Environment.

Working individually on Fund-supported smaller projects, jointly on larger country or regional programmes, executing agencies ensure that the best international technical and professional skills are made available. They recruit experts from all parts of the world, organize seminars and training courses, procure equipment from countries capable of providing timely delivery and contract special services when needed.

In addition to supervising Fund-assisted projects, agency personnel perform an important training function by helping local staff to improve professional skills and acquire modern techniques. They also contribute their advice and expertise, upon request, for other government-sponsored programmes.

Executing agencies provide the link between the Population

Fund and its donor and recipient countries, making each participant part of a common effort, to which all can contribute and from which all can benefit.

UNFPA resources

Although funds are increasing rapidly, urgency of the world's population problems demands still greater fund-raising efforts. The Fund's planners have already charted a four-year budget for 1972-75 totalling over $250 million. By 1974, the level of annual contribution is expected to surpass $100 million.

The Fund is financed by voluntary contributions from governments as well as private donors. Initially, the programme got under way with a small budget contributed by a few countries. But it grew rapidly. By 1970, 24 countries had contributed $15·4 million, and in 1971 alone pledges had reached $28 million, surpassing the target set for that year by $3 million.

Growth was marked in 1971 by voluntary donations from 21 new contributing nations, bringing the total number of donor countries to 45. Largest donor was the United States with $12·5 million on a matching basis, followed by Sweden with $3 million, Canada and Japan with $2 million each, and the Federal Republic of Germany, Norway and United Kingdom with $1·5 million each.

By mid-1972, the list of donors included: Afghanistan, Barbados, Botswana, Canada, Cyprus, Denmark, Dominican Republic, Egypt, Finland, France, Federal Republic of Germany, Greece, Guatemala, Honduras, Hungary, Iceland, India, Indonesia, Iran, Iraq, Jamaica, Japan, Jordan, Lebanon, Lesotho, Liberia, Madagascar, Mauritius, Morocco, Nepal, Netherlands, New Zealand, Norway, Pakistan, Philippines, Singapore, Somalia, Sri Lanka, Swaziland, Sweden, Switzerland, Thailand, Togo, Trinidad & Tobago, Tunisia, United Kingdom, Republic of Vietnam, Yugoslavia and the United States. By mid-1972 there were 74 nations receiving aid from UNFPA.

SOURCE: United Nations Fund for Population Activities

Rafael Salas, its Executive Director, has spoken about UNFPA as follows:

'To my mind, the rapid rise in support for the recently established United Nations Fund for Population Activities, particularly over the last twelve months, is not only indicative of a universal alarm at the world's present population situation but also of a universal determination through urgent combined action to do something about it.'

The Peterson Report, dealing with US foreign aid, recognised that UNFPA and other international bodies would play a major part in investigations into the best methods of dealing with world population growth.

30 Peterson Report
GATHERING DATA

There are no objective standards against which to measure the developing world's total requirements for assistance in the population field. This is an area in international development that could benefit greatly from strong international leadership. A worldwide study, prepared on a priority basis, could give the United States as well as other countries—industrial and developing nations alike—a professional and politically acceptable base for examining the resources needed and the ways in which each country could best contribute to this pressing world problem. The Task Force recommends that the United States propose that the U.N. Fund for Population Activities, in conjunction with the World Bank and other interested international agencies, prepare a careful and detailed study of world needs and potentialities in this area and of ways in which all elements of the international community can help.

SOURCE: *US Foreign Assistance in the 1970s: A New Approach* (The Peterson Report)

United Nations Children's Fund

31A UN
ACTIVITIES OF UNICEF

In recent years UNICEF has been concerned with the effects that high fertility and too rapid and unplanned population growth can have on the welfare and health of mothers and children, as well as on the preparation of children and youth for their subsequent constructive participation in society.

In 1967 the mandate of UNICEF was expanded to include assistance to family planning, as part of maternal and child health services, upon the request of Governments. Based on the recommendations of the UNICEF/WHO Joint Committee on Health Policy, the UNICEF Executive Board decided that, whereas it was not the organization's role to advocate any specific way of dealing with the problems of population growth, support might be extended where a government wished UNICEF assistance. The types of activities for which a country might receive assistance could be those directed at training and supervision in maternal and child health care, including family planning, and those directed at the expansion of basic health services, including maternal and child health care and family planning activities.

Subsequently, it became evident that, although adequate maternal and child health service were essential for a successful family planning scheme, the maternal and child health programme could not carry the whole burden. It needed to be supplemented by whatever services were in touch with the great masses of people for education and motivation, such as the school system, agricultural extension services, community development, social services and the mass media. The Executive Board therefore agreed at its 1970 session that a wider approach to UNICEF participation in family planning might be necessary in the future. At the same time it approved the provision, upon request, of contraceptives.

In addition to participation in family planning programmes, UNICEF may co-operate with national or international research institutes in undertaking studies on problems of children and youth resulting from rapid population growth and in helping to develop statistical information on the situation of young people.

SOURCE: United Nations Children's Fund, New York

Henry Labouisse, Executive Director of UNICEF, explained the organisation's concern with the population increase in the following statement.

'UNICEF is deeply concerned about the population explosion because it is the children who suffer most from the inability of parents to provide sufficient care and attention to their large families—as well as from the difficulty of governments to meet ever growing demands for health, education, welfare and other services.'

United Nations Educational, Scientific and Cultural Organisation

31B UN
UNESCO IN THE POPULATION FIELD

The responsibilities of UNESCO in the field of population, as established by the General Conference in 1968, are mainly in the following three areas: social science studies; integration of various media of mass communication into the educational process; and educational work at formal and out-of-school levels. The mandate of the organization is being carried out not only by promoting research and studies but also by providing fellowships, advisory services, exploratory missions, seminars, training courses and the dissemination of information. Social science studies are in progress on the different aspects of population and family planning to promote better understanding of the complexity of family planning in the context of various cultures. As regards communication, activities are being developed on training in the use of communication media, on the production and promotion of educational materials and on research and evaluation of their effective use and integration in population and family planning programmes. The organization is assisting in the development of relevant teaching materials, curricula, teacher training, adult education, women's education and community education. The possibility of including an educational component on family planning in experimental literacy programmes is being investigated.

SOURCE: United Nations Educational, Scientific and Cultural Organisation, Paris

Food and Agriculture Organisation of the United Nations

31C UN
FAO WORK IN RELATION TO POPULATION

Within the context of its responsibilities in the field of food and agriculture development and raising the levels of nutrition and family living, especially in rural areas, FAO supports policies for attaining moderate and balanced rates of population growth in the developing regions. The FAO Conference held in 1967 recommended that the organization should be increasingly involved in the study of the relations between food supplies and population growth and the interaction between demographic and agricultural changes. It should be prepared to undertake education and training activities in support of national programmes to improve the levels of family living through better utilization of resources. The Conference also approved the carrying out of field programmes, upon request, in planning for better family living, making use of home economics and agricultural extension programmes, specialized programmes for women and youth, and applied nutrition programmes, reaching individual families.

The work of FAO in relation to population comprises (a) research and informational activities concerned with the interrelationships between population trends and agricultural development; (b) population projections for occupational groups directly relevant to agriculture; and (c) the development of a comprehensive educational programme in planning for better family living with family planning as an integral part and comprising studies on communication and training, as well as field activities.

SOURCE: Food and Agriculture Organisation of the United Nations, Rome

OTHER ORGANISATIONS

International Labour Office

32 ILO
POLICY ON POPULATION

The International Labour Conference in 1967 adopted a resolution on the influence of rapid population growth on employment, training and the welfare of workers, with specific reference to developing countries. Following on this resolution, the Governing Body endorsed proposals that the ILO act in support of appropriate national and international efforts to moderate population growth in developing countries.

The following three types of measures are being considered:
(1) Promotion of information and educational activities on population and family planning questions at various levels and particularly through workers' education, labour welfare and co-operative and rural institutions' programmes:
(2) Policy-oriented research on the demographic aspects and measures of social policy in certain fields, such as employment and promotion of social security; and

(3) Action to stimulate participation by social security and by medical services at enterprise level in promotion of family planning.

In addition to its current activities relating to technical work on labour force statistics and manpower studies under the World Employment Programme, the enlarged mandate of the ILO, as outlined above, is in the process of being translated into programmes and projects. The responsibilities of the ILO under existing programmes already provide a basis for it to initiate and develop appropriate action, particularly by creating an awareness of population problems and by promoting support for the implementation of population action programmes through employers' and workers' organizations, social security institutions, industrial medical services and welfare facilities, workers' education programmes, co-operatives and rural institutions.

SOURCE: International Labour Office, Geneva

World Health Organisation

33 WHO
HEALTH AND POPULATION

Since 1965, resolutions adopted by the World Health Assemblies have given WHO a broad mandate to work on the health aspects of human reproduction, of family planning and of population dynamics and to assist member States, on request, in the development of family planning activities in health programmes. This includes the relevant training of all categories of health personnel; and the stimulation, co-ordination and support of research and reference services on administrative, epidemiological, clinical, physiological and psychological aspects of these questions.

The mandate of the organization recognizes that the problems of human reproduction and family planning involve the family unit as well as the community. It emphasizes that the size of the family and the spacing of children are the free choice of each individual family; and reaffirms that all couples should have the opportunity to obtain information and advice on problems relating to family planning. WHO does not endorse or promote any particular population policy but can provide assistance as outlined above within any policy that might be established by individual member States.

A wide range of programme activities in human reproduction, family planning and population dynamics is being developed and expanded by the organization. Advisory services and technical assistance are provided on the organization and administration of family planning—within the context of health services, especially in their nursing and health education aspects, and in the evaluation of programmes.

Special emphasis is being given to training in this as in other areas of health. Activities here are concerned with the inclusion of family planning training in the ongoing WHO educational projects, special short-term training programmes, and the development of suitable curricula to include the subject matter of family planning and population in schools of medicine, nursing and public health. Training manuals and texts for these purposes are being prepared. WHO supports administrative research projects with the aim especially of evaluating the relative merits of different approaches to the provision of family planning in the context of comprehensive health services. The organization supports long-term epidemiological studies of reproductive practices, and of health and population dynamics. Investigations on the physiology of reproduction and on clinical aspects of pregnancy, lactation and fertility regulation are also assisted. Scientific groups are convened to review knowledge of various aspects of human reproduction and make recommendations as to areas requiring further research.

SOURCE: World Health Organisation, Geneva

International Bank for Reconstruction and Development

34 World Bank
ASSISTANCE FOR POPULATION POLICIES

Since 1968, IBRD has taken initiatives in the area of population policies, following studies that have shown the crippling effect of a high rate of population increase on economic growth in developing countries. Several country missions have been sent out to explore how IBRD could assist those countries in the field of population control and to develop action programmes.

The process of assisting developing countries in the formulation and implementation of population policies with the aim of limiting rapid population growth is given practical expression in the recent establishment of a population projects department within the organization. The following areas of activity are under consideration:

Carrying out of research on the relationships between population growth and economic development;

Evaluation, through periodic economic missions, of the effect of population growth in the countries reviewed and stimulation of the development of population policies by making known the analyses of demographic conditions and their economic implications;

Provision of technical advice on implementation of population policies and programmes; and

Provision of finance for implementing family planning and related facilities within the context of the current policies of IBRD.

SOURCE: World Bank (International Bank for Reconstruction and Development), Washington, DC

Two statements by its President, Robert S. McNamara, explain why the World Bank is concerned with population control.

'We are not lending in the field of population because it is less expensive, or because it is less trouble, or because it constitutes in itself an all-purpose formula for economic progress. Lending for population projects is not development-on-the-cheap. Quite the contrary, lending for population is a premium well worth paying in order to help ensure that a country's entire development effort will have a more reasonable chance to succeed.'

'It is important to understand why an institution such as the World Bank is concerned with the population problem. The reason is simple. No other single problem is a greater threat to the prospects for economic and social progress in the developing world. The World Bank is an international development agency, and for it to be indifferent to the inescapable consequences of rampant population growth in the poorer nations would amount to its being indifferent to the larger goal of development itself.'

International Planned Parenthood Federation

35 IPPF
AIMS AND ACHIEVEMENTS

The International Planned Parenthood Federation—founded in 1952—is an international non-governmental organization which believes that knowledge of family planning is a basic human right and that a balance between the population of the world and its natural resources and productivity is a necessary condition of human happiness, prosperity and peace.

The IPPF encourages the formation of national associations to pioneer family planning services in each country of the world and to bring about a favourable climate of public opinion in which governments can be persuaded to accept responsibility. Family planning associations offer contraceptive services, set and maintain high clinical standards, train all levels of personnel, and carry out education programmes to inform and teach

ORGANISATIONS CONCERNED WITH POPULATION PROBLEMS 203

people about the personal, health, social and economic benefits of family planning.

Where governments have already responded to these initiatives by setting up family planning programmes, IPPF-affiliated associations provide a nucleus of experienced staff around which an expanded government programme can be built. As the government gradually develops clinic services, usually based on existing health services, the Association concentrates on education of the general public and training for association and government staff, while often continuing to maintain clinics for both research and training.

With IPPF assistance, many associations are bringing education for responsible parenthood to young people, both in and out of school. They are also reaching industrial and plantation workers and other special groups.

Financial support
As the IPPF's membership has grown, so too has the demand for resources to support its work. In 1961, the budget of the IPPF was US $30,000. By 1971, only 10 years later, the gross budget (including the local income of grant-receiving agencies) had risen to US $20 million, primarily as a result of confidence in the IPPF as a non-governmental body especially qualified to initiate and support the development of family planning services.

The Federation is financed by voluntary contributions from foundations and private citizens all over the world and by grants from governments. In 1971, in addition to the assistance which governments gave directly to their national family planning association, grants were made to the IPPF by Britain, Canada, Denmark, Finland, Japan, Norway, Sweden and the United States, as well as by the United Nations Fund for Population Activities.

Regional activities
For administrative purposes, and in recognition of the wide

diversity of problems that confront its members, the IPPF is divided into seven regions. The regional offices in Beirut, Colombo, Kuala Lumpur, London, Nairobi, New York and Tokyo assist family planning associations in their areas, arrange regional conferences, encourage the establishment of new organizations, sponsor applications for IPPF membership, and submit reports and accounts to the IPPF Governing Body, under the direction of their Regional Councils. Technical assistance and advisory services are provided to the associations by both the IPPF Central Office and the Regional Offices.

Africa
IPPF has stimulated the growth of indigenous organizations in 15 countries of sub-Sahara Africa to establish pilot clinics and to bring about an awareness of health and economic problems associated with social change and an average population growth rate of 2·5%. Four governments have now begun national family planning programmes and have recognized the pioneering work of the voluntary associations by integrating association activities and government programmes. In the remaining 11 countries, there has been a rapid increase in the number of patients served, in some cases four times greater than in the previous year. Despite a desperate shortage of skilled personnel, volunteers have gradually been supported by salaried professionals while regional seminars and workshops have identified common goals, built confidence, and educated opinion leaders. Educational activities, especially films specifically researched and produced for African societies with differing cultures and traditions, have helped boost the number of family planning acceptors. A unique development in the region has been seven IPPF-supported mobile teams in Kenya which provide over one-third of the total clinic services covering a rural population of 3 million people.

Europe
In recent years European governments have begun to accept

greater responsibility for family planning services, and many universities and medical schools today teach contraception and human reproduction. As a result, many European family planning associations act as non-governmental co-ordinating committees, assisting governments in planning and developing family planning services and implementing information and education programmes with greater emphasis on sex education. To supplement income received through their governments and/or through the sale of contraceptives and to assist the developing countries, several associations have begun their own fund raising activities. Five European governments now include family planning in their development assistance overseas and others are interested in doing so.

Indian Ocean
Since governments in the Indian sub-continent are widely involved in clinical services, the family planning associations have increasingly explored new ways of overcoming communications barriers, including the use of mobile units, factory and plantation-based campaigns. Associations have experimented with films and other audio-visual aids, while in India, pioneer work is being carried out to introduce population education into the schools in order to reach the 41% of the population under the age of 15. Because of high illiteracy rates, associations have turned to mass media, especially radio, to motivate the largest possible number of people. Research into past and current work is proving valuable in determining future activities and priorities.

Middle East and North Africa
From a new regional base in Beirut, the IPPF, through seminars and meetings, has drawn attention to high abortion and infant mortality rates and has gained growing government recognition of the contribution which family planning can make to the solution of these problems. One result of the IPPF seminars has been to stimulate research never before done on

fertility trends and national demographic patterns. Family planning associations in seven countries are building educational and clinical activities as pioneers or in support of government programmes.

South-east Asia and Oceania

Pioneer efforts of IPPF-supported family planning associations in 13 countries have brought several governments, representing more than 200 million people, to the policy and implementation stages of national birth control campaigns. In 1970, most training and family planning services in Indonesia and the Philippines were still being provided by voluntary associations. The quality of their work, especially their ability to recruit and train large numbers of fieldworkers to carry out massive rural and urban education campaigns, will be vital factors in the success of governmental programmes.

In the Pacific islands, Thailand and Laos, IPPF assistance has been directed toward stimulating greater governmental involvement, providing training opportunities for doctors, nurses and field staff, and supporting pilot services.

Western Hemisphere

Recent years have witnessed the increased professionalization of family planning associations in Latin America and the Caribbean. Where most associations were formerly completely dependent on volunteer help from doctors, now the majority also have full-time professional staffs, resulting in more efficient administration, long-range planning and budgeting, and the improvement of information and education programmes. Some countries of the Western Hemisphere enjoy a degree of official support but generally governments have been slow to recognize their responsibilities. A number of associations have for the first time initiated local fund-raising campaigns to finance rapidly expanding programmes. Mass media campaigns to motivate women to use family planning are being used in several countries with good results.

Western Pacific

The practice of family planning has risen each year and the population growth rate in the region continues to decline. This remarkable achievement has been the result of close co-operation between governments and IPPF-assisted associations. In Hong Kong, the birth rate has declined from 3·6% in 1961 to 2·1% in 1969, while Korea is within sight of its target to reduce population growth to 2% from a 1960 high of 2·9%. The 13 clinics of the Planned Parenthood Federation of Korea served 32,000 patients in 1969 and the total rose to more than 45,000 for 1970. Women were educated through mothers clubs in 17,000 villages.

SOURCE: International Planned Parenthood Federation, London

Dr Julia Henderson, Secretary-General of the IPPF, defines its aims as follows.

'In a world of nearly 4,000,000,000 people only the United Nations can provide the global perspective and world leadership that will be necessary to resolve the population problem and to raise the quality of life for all people.

The International Planned Parenthood Federation looks confidently forward to such leadership from the United Nations family. IPPF in turn pledges its full cooperation and assistance in undertakings with each of the United Nations agencies to bring to all of the couples in the world the basic human right of voluntary, rational, and responsible control over human reproduction.'

The IPPF expressed its philosophy in the following statement, made to the UN Conference on the Human Environment.

'... Within the compass of the single nation it could never be appropriate for a rich minority to instruct a poor majority to control its fertility as though this by itself would solve the problems of society. Within the context of a single planet, a village world, such an attitude is equally inappropriate.'

Organisation for Economic Cooperation and Development (OECD)

36 OECD
WORK ON POPULATION

In 1968 the OECD Development Centre was authorised to undertake certain activities in the field of population, in order to:
—draw attention to the importance of the population factor in development;
—promote the exchange of information in the field;
—help the Development Assistance Committee to co-ordinate aid programmes; and
—promote a dialogue between aid donors and recipients on aid problems.

Since its creation, the OECD Population Unit has pursued these objectives by organizing conferences, undertaking a limited amount of applied research, and by building up a network of contacts of international, governmental and non-governmental organisations working in population. A library on population matters has been created and indexed, and a world-wide mailing list has been built for the circulation of a mimeographed information sheet entitled 'OECD Population Abstracts' which contains abstracts of new publications on population and information about the Unit's activities, proceedings and results of meetings.

SOURCE: Population Unit, Development Centre of the OECD, Paris

Population Council

37 Population Council
AIMS

The Population Council was established in November 1952 'to stimulate, encourage, promote, conduct and support significant activities in the broad field of population'. The Council, a private foundation, seeks to advance and apply knowledge by fostering research, training, and technical assistance in the social and biomedical sciences.

Its objectives are:

—to study the problems presented by the increasing population of the world and the relation of that population to material and cultural resources;

—to encourage and support research and to disseminate as appropriate the knowledge resulting from such research;

—to serve generally as a centre for the collection and exchange of facts and information on the significant ideas and developments relating to population questions;

—to co-operate with individuals and institutions in the development of programmes;

—to take initiative in the broad fields which in the aggregate constitute the population problem.

Budget: $16,000,000—1970

SOURCE: Population Council, New York

Rockefeller Foundation

38 Rockefeller Foundation
WORK ON POPULATION

The Foundation started activities in the population field in 1963. Since then the main part of the $22·2 million population funds (62%) has been used for action programmes, such as supporting Population Council's technical assistance division, establishing family planning units in medical schools both in the U.S. and in developing countries, integrating family planning in community health services (e.g. in Colombia and India) and supporting Planned Parenthood of America in establishing a Centre for Family Planning Programme Development.

The Rockefeller Foundation is concentrating its population activities increasingly on the interaction of the social, medical and biological sciences. In 1970, 77% of the population allocations was committed to research in reproductive biology and contraceptive development, and 22% to training, research and development in population/family planning. Apart from support for universities in the U.S.A., recent Rockefeller grants have been made to universities in Chile, Colombia, Mexico, Thailand, Turkey and the United Kingdom.

Obligations: US $15,000,000—1970

SOURCE: Rockefeller Foundation, New York

The following statement by John D. Rockefeller 3rd, chairman of the Population Council and the Rockefeller Foundation, exemplifies the need for government action.

'Private groups can contribute much in the way of information, specialized knowledge and trained personnel, but population problems are so great, so important, so ramified and often so immediate, that only government, supported and inspired by private initiative, can attack them on the scale required . . . To my mind population growth is second only to the control of atomic weapons as the paramount problem of our day . . .'

Ford Foundation

39 Ford Foundation
EXPENDITURE ON POPULATION STUDIES

Foundation expenditures in population began modestly in 1952 and have grown to a substantial magnitude ever since. Over the past sixteen years the Ford Foundation has devoted US $132 million to work directed to world population problems. However, population expenditures in 1968 only amounted to about six per cent of the Foundation's total commitments. Slightly more than half of the Foundation's population commitments have been directed to research and training in reproductive biology ($72 million), the balance for training and research in other aspects of population and family planning, for dissemination of information on population problems.

About two-thirds of the Foundation's expenditures in population have gone to American institutions, although the activities supported by these grants are primarily directed toward population problems in developing countries.

In population, as in the case of its other development assistance activities, the Foundation is both a grant-making and an operating agency. The Foundation has made substantial funds available to the Population Council ($30 million since 1954) through general support grants, as well as grants for specific technical assistance programmes in such countries as Pakistan and Ceylon.

Commitments: $15,000,000—1970

SOURCE: Ford Foundation, New York

International Union for the Scientific Study of Population

40 IUSSP
AIMS

The International Union for the Scientific Study of Population was founded in 1928, Paris.

Aims:

Advance the progress of quantitative and qualitative demography as a science, through publications, by organizing congresses, by furthering relationships between demographers of all countries; stimulate interest in demography among countries and among national and international institutions originating in such countries, as well as in the scientific and intellectual world, and the general public.

SOURCE: International Union for the Scientific Study of Population, Liége

The scale of assistance for development and population planning throughout the world is given in Tables 12, 13 and 14.

TABLE 12

Assistance for demographic, biomedical and family planning work, by regions, 1969 and 1970*

Thousand US dollars

Purpose	Near-East and South-East Asia Region	East Asia	Africa	Latin America	Oceania	International and other	Total
1969:							
Demography	961·2	161·9	1,193·0	8,168·9	—	703·0	11,187·9
Biomedical	309·3	106·5	50·1	1,438·3	235·2	350·0	2,489·3
Family Planning	21,176·0	2,704·9	3,960·5	4,463·1	16·7	2,741·1	35,062·3
Other	341·1	14·5	151·8	14·8	—	306·5	828·7
Total	22,787·6	2,987·8	5,355·4	14,085·1	251·9	4,100·6	49,568·3
1970:							
Demography	2,816·3	228·1	1,379·6	8,859·3	11·9	1,205·3	14,500·5
Biomedical	251·6	71·1	157·6	1,147·4	40·0	427·6	2,095·3
Family Planning	44,849·0	2,325·4	6,848·4	5,659·5	39·3	1,141·5	60,863·0
Other	188·9	163·5	253·5	1,263·4	—	513·9	2,383·3
Total	48,105·7	2,788·2	8,639·1	16,929·6	91·1	3,288·4	79,842·2

* Excluding administrative costs.

Source: OECD

TABLE 13

Assistance to population activities as percentage of total official development assistance, 1969 and 1970

DAC countries	Official development assistance $ million	1969 Assistance to population activities* $ thousand	As percentage of official development assistance	Official development assistance $ million	1970 Assistance to population activities* $ thousand	As percentage of official development assistance
Australia	174·6	..	..	203·4	..	..
Austria	15·5	..	..	19·1	..	..
Belgium	116·1	..	..	119·6	10·0	—
Canada	245·2	..	..	346·3	..	..
Denmark	54·3	296·2	0·55	59·1	1,349·0	2·28
France	955·2	..	..	951·1	..	..
Germany	579·3	250·0	0·04	599·0	1,525·0	0·25
Italy	129·6	..	..	147·2	..	..
Japan	435·6	198·8	0·05	458·0	377·8	0·08
Netherlands	143·1	338·0	0·24	196·4	1,408·0	0·72
Norway	29·5	225·3	0·76	36·8	990·0	2·69
Portugal	58·3	..	..	28·5	..	..
Sweden	120·5	5,473·8	4·54	117·0	6,311·0	5·39
Switzerland	29·5	..	..	29·4	..	..
United Kingdom	431·3	261·4†	0·06	447·1	351·1	0·08
United States	3,092·0	45,440·0	1·47	3,050·0	58,341·0	1·91
Total DAC countries	6,609·6	52,483·4	0·79	6,808·0	70,662·9	1·04
Finland		50·0			75·0	

* Excluding administrative costs. Refers to amounts provided by each donor and to multilateral agencies.
† Referring to Fiscal Year.

Source: OECD

Table 14
Resources provided to assist population activities, by region, 1970*

	Near-East and South-East Asia	East Asia	Africa	Latin America	Oceania	Other	Thousands of US dollars Total
Donor Countries	34,198·2	1,363·7	4,288·9	7,570·6	5·8	386·9	47,814·1
Multilateral Agencies and Other	13,907·5	1,424·5	4,350·2	9,359·0	85·4	2,901·6	32,028·2
	48,105·7	2,788·2	8,639·1	16,929·6	91·2	3,288·5	79,842·3

* Excluding Administrative Costs.

SOURCE: OECD

APPENDIX 1

Definitions

CONCEPTION CONTROL

This may be defined as all the means—*behavioural, mechanical, chemical, physiological and surgical*—*by which conception is prevented. Sheldon J. Segal, PhD, vice-president and director, Bio-Medical Division, the Population Council, and Christopher Tietze, MD, associate director, have provided the following 'introduction' to the subject of contraceptive technology.*

CONTRACEPTIVE TECHNOLOGY

Until recently, the scientific basis of most contraceptive methods was the realization that the ejaculate represents or contains the male factor responsible for fertilization. For centuries, mankind attempted to prevent pregnancy by the simple and direct procedure of withdrawing the penis prior to ejaculation; by mechanical devices such as the condom, and, later, the diaphragm; by a variety of chemical spermicides introduced into the vagina; and retroactively by post-coital douching. The effectiveness, or lack of it, of these procedures depends on their success in preventing sperm from making their way to the arena of fertilization, the fallopian tubes, on the occasion of a particular coitus. Permanent blockage of sperm passage was achieved by surgical procedures on the male and female genital organs.

Contraceptive technology caught up with the twentieth century when scientists turned their attention to the ovulatory cycle in the female and the hormonal control of reproduction in both sexes. The principle of periodic abstinence timed to avoid coitus near the day of ovulation was the first method of fertility regulation that had as its basis a modern scientific understanding of the reproductive process. That the rhythm method has never proven to be an effective contraceptive practice does not detract from its significance in focusing upon the ovulatory process as a key event for control of fertility. It was several decades before the necessary knowledge was marshalled to develop effective means to prevent ovulation, but when that moment came, the practice of contraception was revolutionized. The era of hormonal contraception was launched and, with it, the search for different ways to achieve the regulation of fertility by interfering with specific links in the reproductive chain of events.

Almost without exception, experimental efforts to inhibit fertility can be described as attempts to manipulate a key event in the endocrine control of reproduction. With the gradual elucidation of the normal hormonal requirements of the reproductive process, it becomes apparent that there are many steps in this sequence that are vulnerable to controlled interference.

SOURCE: Population Council, *Studies in Family Planning* (January 1968)

BIRTH CONTROL

This includes conception control, and, in addition, abortion, the elimination of the product of conception before birth.

POPULATION CONTROL

This form of control involves not only birth control, but also the relationship between fertility, mortality and net migration (the balance between immigration and emigration and internal in-migration and out-migration). It also takes into account the effects of social, economic and political changes on population growth.

Population policies cannot be considered separately from broader questions of development. A high level of social and economic development has universally been accompanied by a reduction in natality. With major socio-economic changes, an increasing number of less developed countries are experiencing reductions in fertility. There have been important breakthroughs in the cultural and climatic barriers to spread of lower birth rates

Population planning and development must proceed hand-in-hand. Without reduction in the rate of population growth, economic development may be severely jeopardised. At the same time, without economic development, and without a radical transformation in the structures of society, reduction in the rate of population growth will be hard to achieve; nor, by itself, will it solve the problem of poverty.

All government policies aimed at economic growth and social development will affect fertility. But several specific governmental policies and programs which have improvement in welfare as a primary objective will also lower the benefits and increase the costs of having children, and they may therefore be considered policies for limiting fertility.

Educational and employment opportunities for young women give them an alternative to early marriage and childbearing.

By widening their horizons and circles of communication, one may enable women to obtain better information on means of limiting their own fertility.

Considerable reduction in death rate is possible through improvements in nutrition, inoculations against infectious disease and other public health measures. When average infant and child mortalities are high, the uncertainty faced by individual parents concerning the number of their children who are likely to survive is also high. Parents may compensate for this uncertainty by accepting the cost of having 'extra' children. Policies and programmes aimed at reducing infant and child mortality below present levels, therefore, may be an essential underpinning of governmental programmes for fertility control.

Social security, old-age insurance and pensions can reduce the economic incentive for having children. Similarly, compulsory education and prohibition of child labour may also reduce the benefits and increase the costs of having children, thus influencing fertility.

APPENDIX 2

Thomas Robert Malthus (1766-1834)

It is one of the stranger turns of history that the 'population explosion'—an event which perhaps more than any other has come to dominate the second half of the twentieth century—is almost inevitably linked in the popular mind with an eighteenth-century English country parson, Thomas Robert Malthus. In *1798*, in his first Essay on the Principle of Population, *Malthus put forward the proposition that the 'power of population is indefinitely greater than the power in the earth to produce subsistence. . . . Population, when unchecked, increases in a geometrical ratio. Subsistence increases only in an arithmetical ratio.' Malthus added to, and modified, the* Essay *in subsequent years. The introduction of the notion of 'moral restraint' (today it might be called 'responsible parenthood'), which could provide some kind of a check on population increase, gave a slightly more hopeful tinge to later editions of his famous work. The alternative, as Malthus saw it, was positive checks of the kind which had operated in the past—famine, pestilence and war—with all that this implied for the future of mankind.*

Malthus's father, Daniel, was an associate of David Hume and both friend and executor of Jean-Jacques Rousseau. It was his father who encouraged him, once he had completed his studies at Cambridge and had taken up the curacy at Albury, to publish the Essay. *In 1805 Malthus married and took up a post at the East India Company's college at*

Haileybury. Himself one of eight children, Malthus in turn fathered three. Besides his work on population, he was a noted economist and a close friend of David Ricardo. He died at Haileybury on 23 December 1834.

World population has increased fourfold since Malthus died. Food production still manages (barely) to stay ahead of population growth. Was Malthus right or wrong?

SOURCE: *The Sunday Times*

Bibliography

A Population growth

THE AMERICAN ASSEMBLY. *The Population Dilemma*, edited by Philip M. Hauser, 2nd ed (1969)

BEAUJEU-GARNIER, J. *Geography of Population*, translated by S. H. Beaver (1966)

BORRIE, W. D. *The Growth and Control of World Population* (1970)

EHRLICH, PAUL R. *The Population Bomb* (New York, 1971), bibliography

FISHER, TADD. *Our Overcrowded World* (New York, 1969)

LORAINE, JOHN A. *Sex and the Population Crisis: an Endocrinologist's View of the 20th Century* (1970)

McCORMACK, ARTHUR. *The Population Problem* (New York, 1970)

SHELESNYAK, M. C. (ed). *Growth of Population: Consequences and Controls: Proceedings of the 1st Conference on Population, Princeton, NJ, September 1968* (New York, 1969)

SOCIETY FOR THE STUDY OF HUMAN BIOLOGY. *Biological Aspects of Demography: Symposia of the Society for the Study of Human Biology*, vol X, edited by William Brass (1971)

UNITED NATIONS. *Growth of the World's Urban and Rural Population, 1920–2000*. Population Studies, No 44 (New York, 1969)

UNITED NATIONS ASSOCIATION OF THE US. *World Population: A Challenge to the United Nations and Its system of Agencies* (1969)

UNITED STATES NATIONAL ACADEMY OF SCIENCES. *Rapid Population Growth* (1972)

Regional and country studies on the population problem
BIRTH CONTROL CAMPAIGN. *A Birth Control Plan for Britain* (Southwick, Sussex, 1972)
COUNCIL ON POPULATION AND ENVIRONMENT. *Population, Environment and People*, edited by Noel Hinrichs (New York, 1971)
POPULATION REFERENCE BUREAU. 'Where will the Next 50 Million Americans Live?', *The Population Bulletin*, vol 27, no 5 (October 1971)
REGIER, HENRY and FALLS, J. BRUCE (eds). *Exploding Humanity: the Crisis of Numbers* (Toronto, 1969)
TAYLOR, L. R. (ed). 'The Optimum Population for Britain', *Proceedings of the Institute of Biology Symposium in London, 25 and 26 September 1969* (1970)

B Family planning in the context of population and the environment

PLANNED PARENTHOOD—WORLD POPULATION. *When More Is Less: An Economic Examination of World Population and Family Planning Programme* (New York, 1968)
STYCOS, J. MAYONE. *Ideology, Faith and Family Planning in Latin America* (New York, 1971)
UNITED NATIONS. *Human Fertility and National Development: A Challenge to Science and Technology* (New York, 1971)
WORLD EDUCATION INC. *Literacy and Family Planning* (New Haven, Conn, 1969)

C The environment

ALLABY, MICHAEL. *The Eco-Activists* (1971)
COMMONER, BARRY. *The Closing Circle: Confronting the Environmental Crisis* (1972)
THE CONSERVATION SOCIETY. *United Nations Conference on the Human Environment, 1972* (1972)

DE BELL, GARRETT (ed). *The Environmental Handbook* (New York, 1970)
THE ECOLOGIST. *A Blueprint for Survival*, vol II, no 1 (January 1972)
EHRLICH, PAUL R. and HARRIMAN, RICHARD L. *How to Be a Survivor* (1971)
EHRLICH, PAUL R. and ANNE. *Population, Resources and Environment* (1972)
HELFRICH, HAROLD W., JR (ed). *Agenda for Survival: The Environmental Crisis—2* (New Haven, 1971)
HELFRICH, HAROLD W., JR (ed). *The Environmental Crisis: Man's Struggle to Live with Himself* (New Haven, 1970)
INSTITUTE OF DEVELOPMENT STUDIES. *Bulletin* (University of Sussex, December 1971)
LOVE, GLEN A. and RHODA M. *Ecological Crisis: Readings for Survival* (New York, 1970)
TAYLOR, GORDON R. *The Doomsday Book* (1970)
URBAN, G. R. and GLENNY, MICHAEL (eds). *Can We Survive Our Future?* (1971)

D Food resources

DARLING, FRANK FRASER. *Wilderness and Plenty*, the Reith Lectures, 1969 (1970)
DUMONT, RÉNE and ROSIER, BERNARD. *The Hungry Future* (1969)
HUTCHINSON, SIR JOSEPH (ed). *Population and Food Supply* (1969)
PADDOCK, WILLIAM C. 'How Green Is the Green Revolution?', *Bioscience*, vol 20, no 16 (15 August 1970)
CALDER, NIGEL. *The Environment Game* (1967)
INTERNATIONAL COUNCIL ON SOCIAL WELFARE. *Urbanisation, Its Social Problems and Consequences* (Nairobi, 1969)
JOHNSON, STANLEY. *Life without Birth* (1970)
KLAUSNER, SAMUEL Z. *On Man in His Environment* (San Francisco, 1971)
SCIENTIFIC AMERICAN. *Science, Conflict and Society*. Readings from the *Scientific American* (San Francisco, 1969)

E Population education

ARTHUR, DON R. *Survival: Man and His Environment* (1969)
BOUGHEY, ARTHUR S. *Man and the Environment: An Introduction to Human Ecology and Evolution* (New York, 1971)
HANSON, W. J. *Hong Kong: The Overcrowded Room* (1969)
HAZEN, WILLIAM E. (ed). *Readings in Population and Community Ecology*, 2nd ed (Philadelphia, 1970)
LARSEN, TORBEN B. *Befolkningseksplosionen* (Copenhagen, 1969)
LAUWERYS, J. A. *Man's Impact on Nature* (1969)
LAWTON, DENIS (ed). *Population Education and the Younger Generation* (1971)
UNIVERSITY OF DELAWARE. *A Sourcebook for Population-Environment Studies* (Newark, Delaware, 1972)
VOLUNTARY COMMITTEE ON OVERSEAS AID AND DEVELOPMENT— THE EDUCATION UNIT. *The Development Puzzle*, edited by Nancy Lui Fyson, 3rd ed (1972)

SOURCE: IPPF

Index

In this index the abbreviation *HV* is adopted for the Papal Encyclical on Population Control of 1968, *Humanae Vitae*; the word 'Catholic' means the Church of Rome.

The United Nations Fund for Public Activities, popularly called The Planning Fund, is referred to as UNFPA.

The initials IPPF are used for the International Planned Parenthood Federation.

Abortion: the Catholic view, 138; in China, 76; in Latin America, 100; in place of contraception, 105; rate in Chile, 100; where foetus less than 12 weeks, 121; and Islam, 165, 167–8
Abortion legalised in Romania: its effects, 120–8; policy reversed, 124–8
Acauan, Antonio *and* Margarida, 147
Addeke, Boerma, 146
Africa, family planning in, 90–9
Africa, North, IPPF work in, 204
African nuclear families, 93
Agricultural products, the need to increase, 22
Albania, reaction to *HV*, 141
Al-Qalqili, Sheikh Abdullah, 163–6
American scientists' (2,600) view of *HV*, 146
Asia: IPPF work in, 206; UNFPA work in, 183–4; worst problem in, 74–81
'Ask any woman!' (Hart), 156–7

Athenagoras I, view of *HV*, 155
Average age lowering in world, 34–7

Babies, more surviving, 25
Baby Boom or Baby Bust (USA), 119
Beirut Conference (1968), 148
Beliefs, important variable, affecting births, 94
Benjamin, Dr, 109
Berelson, Dr, 33
Bibliography, 221–4
Biosphere, scarce resources of, 58
Birth control defined, 217
Blake, Dr Carson, 156
Blue Print for Survival, A, 67
Borlaug, Dr Norman E., 50–1
Bosch, Juan, 142
Botswana, family planning in, 90–1
Brazilian view of *HV*, 147–8
Bulgaria, where birth rate unusually low, 105–6

Camara, Bishop Helder, 142

Canada abrogates laws forbidding contraception, 106
Capital to be constant, the need for, investment and depreciation to be equal, 70–1
Caracas Declaration, 100–3
Carbon dioxide increasing, 62
Carrill-Flores, Don Antonio, 32
Catholic reaction to *HV*, 140
Catholic view of family planning, 28, 140
Cause of the crisis (India's view), 66
Census programme in Africa, 183
Center for International Documentation on the contemporary Church (IDO-C), 140
Chartier, Michael, 150
Chauchard, Paul, 151
Childlessness Tax (Romania), 125
Children and population growth, 195–6
Children, reasons for wanting, 25, 93–4
Chilean view of population growth, 104
Chile, UNFPA work in, 189
China, family planning in, 75–80
Coitus interruptus and Islam, 165–6
Colombia: view of population growth, 104; reaction to *HV*, 141
Commission on Population Growth (USA), 110–20
Communism and birth control, 157–62
Conception Control Methods defined, 216–17
Concise Summary of the World Population, A (UN), 72
Conjugal act, two aspects of in Catholic view, 136–7
Conjugal love, Catholic view of, 134–5
Conscience in birth control, the problem of, 156
Conservation Society (UK), 109
Constant fertility rate, 37

Contraception, 24
Contraception, A History of Its Treatment by Catholic Theologians and Canonists (Noonan), 153
Contraception limited to intercourse during infecund periods, 139
Countries having official population policies, listed, 23
Countries providing family planning assistance, listed, 23
Cuba, reaction to *HV*, 141

David (1970), 124
Death rate falling, 19–20, 52
Declaration on the Human Environment, 63–4
Demographers and *HV*, 145–9
Demographic Goals, 24–7, 64, 102, 114, 118, 145–9, 176, 180
Determination of family size discussed in China before marriage, 79
Developing world, the, 72–104
Dignity and worth as a quality of life, 115
Doctrinal (Catholic) principles, 133–39
Dutch bishops' attitude to *HV*, 144

Early man described, 17
Ecological balance endangered by urbanisation, 54
Ecologist, The (Jan 1972), 67
Ecology, shall we be too late to master?, 62
Economists and *HV*, 145–9
Ecumenical view on *HV*, 155–6
Education, 196–7; in developing regions, 51; in less developed countries, 51; problems in low income countries, 22
Egypt, UNFPA work in, 186
Emancipation of women (in China) a prerequisite for mass family planning, 77

Employment opportunities must increase as population does, 56–7
Employment problem of finding enough by AD 2000, 57
Engels, Friedrich, 157, 162
Environments, effects on by population growth, 57–8
Equilibrium, the need for a constancy of, 67–71
Ernakulam District Sterilisation Camp (India), 80–8
Europe, IPPF work in, 204–5
Extended family system in Africa, 93

Facts, figures and their meaning, 34–71
Fagley, Richard, 148
Family as basic unit of society, 46–7
Family, need for good spacing in, 61
Family planning, 24, 72; better than abortion, 100; festivals (India), 80–8; in China, 75–80; in Islam, 163–8; promotion of as a human right, 29; (Latin America) fear it is substitute for financial aid, 102
Far East, UNFPA work in, 183–4
Ferenbac, 127
Fertility compared to mortality, 20–1
Fertility rates classed as high, medium and low, 37, 39–40
Flower device (in contraception), 79
Food and Agriculture Organisation index, 21; of the UN (FAO), 197–8
Food in relation to population growth, 47–51, 197–8
Ford Foundation, 211
France abrogates laws forbidding contraception, 106

Gallo, Hubnar, 149
Gandhi, Indira, 64–7, 88
Gandhi, Mahatma, 64
Gedda, Luigi, 151

Géraud, R., 150
Ghana, family planning in, 91
Gheorghiu *et al*, 122
Glass, Professor, 108
Gracias, Cardinal (of India), 141
Grasset, Pierre, 150
'Green revolution', 47, 50–1, 57
Gross Domestic Product (GDP), 59

Hanley, Father Dexter, 148
Han Suyin, 75–80
Hart, Judith, 156
Hauser, Philip M., 180–1
Health, need for increased services for, 51–3
Henderson, Dr Julia, 33
Hernandez, German Zea, 141
Higher living standards with lower birth rate, argument for, 26
Hoffmann, Paul, 29
Homo Sapiens, 17
House of Commons (UK) Select Committee on Science and Technology (1971), 106–10
Housing needs to meet population growth, 54–6
Housing, when health poor, 53
Humanae Vitae, 30; bishops opposing listed, 145; churches supporting listed, 155; criticised by theologians, list of people against, 152–3; extracts from, 130–56; international reactions to, 140–57
Human conscience to have last word, list of countries accepting, 144
Hungary: abortion rate (1958), 122; where birth rate unusually low, 105–6
Hunger, 47

Incentives for sterilisation (India), 84–6
Incentives to increase family size (Romania), 125
Incomes *per capita* compared, 23
Incomes, growth of, 59–60

India: family planning in, 88–90; 1st five-year plan (1951–6), 88; 2nd five-year plan (1956–61), 89; 3rd five-year plan, (1961–6), 89–90; IPPF work in, 205; reaction to *HV*, 141; vasectomy in, 80–8; work of UNFPA in, 187
Indonesia, work of UNFPA in, 187
Infant mortality (China), 78–9
International Bank for Reconstruction and Development, 142
International Conference on Environmental Future, 128–9
International Labour Office (ILO), 198–9
International Union for the Scientific Study of Population (1928) IUSSP), 212
Intra-uterine contraceptive device, 79
Introduction, 17–33
IPPF, 24, 29, 33, 90, 202–8; aims defined, 207; funds available for, 203; regional offices of, 203–4
Iran, UNFPA work in, 187–8
Irrigation schemes for more food, 48
Islam and family planning, 163–8

Janssen, Louis, 147
Japan, reaction to *HV*, 141
Journet, Cardinal (of Switzerland), 145
Justicia et Pax, 148

Kautsky, 157
Kenya, family planning in *and* estimates of population in AD 2000, 92–3
Koch, Dr Ulrich, 149
Koran, The, 163–6

Labouisse, Henry, 196
Labour needs with growth, 56–7, 198–9
Land reclamation for more food, 48

Latin America: a view on *HV*, 148; population growth among world's highest, 100–4; UNFPA work in, 184–5
Leger, Cardinal (of Canada), 145
Lenin, 162
'Let the masses educate themselves' (Thoughts of Mao), 80
Limits to Growth (Report of the Club of Rome), 67–71
Live births compared, 19

McCormack, Arthur, 148
McIntyre, Cardinal (of USA), 145
McNamara, Robert, 142, 201–2
Magisterium, 131–3, 136
Malnutrition, 47, 53
Malthusianism rejected (in China), 77–8, 157
Malthus, Thomas Robert, 219–20
Mao Tse-tung, Chairman, 80
Marriage, average age at: in Africa, 95; in China, 80; delayed as means of non-conception (in China), 79
Martius, Professor Gerhardt, 149
Marxism and birth control, 157–62
Mastboom, James, 151
Mauritius, UNFPA work in, 188
Medical views on *HV*, 149–52
Mehlan (1965), 120–2
Middle East: IPPF work in, 205–6; UNFPA work in, 184

Nasser, President Gamal A., 168
National Population Panel (USA), 61
Nature, meaning of, discussed in *HV*, 154
Neo-Malthusianism, 157–8
Nickolson, Robert, 151
Nixon, Richard M., 176–7
Noonan, John, 153
Nortman, Dorothy, 72
Notta, Julio, 149
Nuclear family system in Africa, 93

O'Boyle, Cardinal (of USA), 145
Okediji, Dr Francis Olu, 90, 93–6
Oraison, Mark, 154
Organisation for Economic Cooperation and Development (OECD), 208
Organisation of American States (OAS), 100, 147
Ottuli, Emil, 151

Pan American Health Organisation (PAHO), 100
Papal Commission *Justitia et Pax*, 148
Parenthood: *see* IPPF; *also* 135–6
Parents' right to determine number and spacing of family, 46–7, 61, 91
Pearson Commission (1969), 60
Petersen Report (US foreign aid), 194
Philippine reaction to *HV*, 141
Philippines, UNFPA work in, 188
Philosophers' views on *HV*, 152–5
Pill, the oral contraceptive, 79, 142–3
Pithecanthropus, 17
Poisonous pesticides, indescriminate use of, 63
Pollution: and health, 53; industrial, 58
Pope Paul VI, views of, 30, 130–56
Population and Family Planning Programmes: A Fact Book (Nortman), 72
Population: awareness, 31; control campaigns, 25–6; control defined, 217–18; Conferences (1954 and 1965), 170; Council, aims of the (1952), 209; crisis, a matter for world concern, 61–2; doubling itself, a table of for percentage growth, 48; estimates of in AD 2000, 37–40, 91
Population Fund, the, 29–30, 32, 181; assistance given to, 182; donors to listed, 193; how it works, 189–90; organisations funded by, listed, 192; project costs tabled, 185–6; resources for, 193–4; world organisations, table of allocation of funds to, 191; *see also* UNFPA
Population growth: comparisons over ½m years, 17, 34, 50, 174; UN Resolution (1966), 171–3
Population, compared in Algeria, Brazil, Ghana, India, Pakistan, Yemen, 21
Population increases expected by AD 2000, discussed, 40–6; daily increase today, 17, 19; in relation to food needs, 47–50; policy (of the UN), 169–70; problem in USA, 112–20; resource equation, 22; Portugal reaction to *HV*, 141
Poverty and health, 53
Profit motives, 66
Puerto Rico's specialist views on *HV*, 147
Pugwash Conference (1971), 128

Quality of Life defined, 115–16

Rabat Conference on Family Planning, 166–8
Radio-active waste, 63
Reductions in death rate, 19–20, 52
Registrar-General (UK) keeps tabs, 108
Religion and Fertility, 28, 30, 95; *see also Humanae Vitae*
Report of the UK Royal Commission on Population (1944); were their conclusions wrong?, 107
Reproduction as a rationality rather than tradition or chance, 118
Resources being squandered, 31
Responsible Parenthood, the Catholic view of, 135–6

Rockefeller Foundation (1963), 209–10
Rockefeller, John D. (3rd), 61, 110–11, 177, 210
Romania, where birth rate unusually low, 105–6, 120–9
Rostow, Walt, 27

Salas, Rafael, 29, 189, 194
Self-control to prevent conception, (in China), 79
Sexual intercourse when lactating will poison the child (African belief), 94
Snijders, Jan, 150
Socialism and birth control, 157–62
Soil erosion, 62
Soviet Union: and birth control, 157–62; a view on *HV*, 148–9
Spain, reaction to *HV*, 141
Speransky, George, 148–9
Sporken, C. P., 150
Stability, society's need for, especially in population, 67–71, 115
Statement of Heads of State on Population Growth (30 signatories), 174–6
Stela, Arias, 143
Sterilisation Camps (in India), 81
Sterilisation, the Catholic view, 138
Subsidies towards family planning, 106
Synod of Bishops (1969), 143
Synthetic detergents, 62

Tanzania, family planning in, by radio, 96–8
Teheran Conference on Human Rights (1968), 47, 176
Thailand, UNFPA work in, 188–9
Theologians' views on *HV*, 152–5
Therapeutic means, the Catholic view of the licitness of, 139
Tisserant, Cardinal (France), 145
Transmission of life, a duty to make, 130
Traverso, Adriano Buzzeti, 146–7

Uganda, family planning in, by radio, 99
Under-employment in low income countries, 22
Under-population, also a problem, 79, 105–6
UNFPA, 181–94; committee members listed, 190; *see also* Population Fund
United Kingdom: densities of population in, 106–7; permits use of contraceptives, 106; problem for the Prime Minister, 110
United Nations: Children's Fund (UNICEF), 195–6; Conference on Human Environment (1972), 63; countries opposing action of, 28; the first Development Decade, (1960–70), 27, 54; Educational, Scientific and Cultural Organisation (UNESCO), 196–7; Human Rights Conference (1968), *see* Teheran; population division, 23, 27, 39–46; population index, 21; Trust Fund for Population (1967), 29
United States legalises the use of contraceptives, 106
United States, the current views set out, 112–20
Universal Declaration of Human Rights, 46–7
Unplanned pregnancies, the social an economic effects of, 46
Urbanisation, today's tendency towards, 53–4, 95
Urlanis, Professor B. Z., 157–62
U Thant, 46–7, 173–4.

Vasectomy, 24, 80–8
Vatican views: *see Humanae Vitae*
Venezuela Declaration, 100–3
Von Geusan, Dr Leo Alting, 140

Waste, problem of disposal of solid, 58
Water supplies, contamination of through increasing sewage, 57, 62
Western hemisphere, IPPF work in, 206
Western Pacific, IPPF work in, 207
Women of China active in education for family planning, 76
Working population, average age of reducing, 56
World Bank: assistance for population policies, 201–2; Population Projects Department, 29–30, 33, 59–61
World Council of Churches, 148, 156
World Health Assembly, 27
World Health Organisation, 199–200
World Population situation (1970), a summary of, 105–6
World Population Year, 32, 180; main objectives of (5), 177

Yugoslavia legalises use of contraceptives, 106

Zuckerman, Sir Solly, 108–9